CLIMATE CHANGE ACTION PLAN 2023–2030

NOVEMBER 2023

ASIAN DEVELOPMENT BANK

Creative Commons Attribution 3.0 IGO license (CC BY 3.0 IGO)

© 2023 Asian Development Bank (ADB)
6 ADB Avenue, Mandaluyong City, 1550 Metro Manila, Philippines
Tel +63 2 8632 4444; Fax +63 2 8636 2444
www.adb.org

Some rights reserved. Published in 2023.

ISBN 978-92-9270-458-2 (print); 978-92-9270-459-9 (electronic); 978-92-9270-460-5 (ebook)
Publication Stock No. SPR230536-2
DOI: http://dx.doi.org/10.22617/SPR230536-2

The views expressed in this publication are those of the authors and do not necessarily reflect the views and policies of the Asian Development Bank (ADB) or its Board of Governors or the governments they represent.

ADB does not guarantee the accuracy of the data included in this publication and accepts no responsibility for any consequence of their use. The mention of specific companies or products of manufacturers does not imply that they are endorsed or recommended by ADB in preference to others of a similar nature that are not mentioned.

By making any designation of or reference to a particular territory or geographic area, or by using the term "country" in this publication, ADB does not intend to make any judgments as to the legal or other status of any territory or area.

This publication is available under the Creative Commons Attribution 3.0 IGO license (CC BY 3.0 IGO) https://creativecommons.org/licenses/by/3.0/igo/. By using the content of this publication, you agree to be bound by the terms of this license. For attribution, translations, adaptations, and permissions, please read the provisions and terms of use at https://www.adb.org/terms-use#openaccess.

This CC license does not apply to non-ADB copyright materials in this publication. If the material is attributed to another source, please contact the copyright owner or publisher of that source for permission to reproduce it. ADB cannot be held liable for any claims that arise as a result of your use of the material.

Please contact pubsmarketing@adb.org if you have questions or comments with respect to content, or if you wish to obtain copyright permission for your intended use that does not fall within these terms, or for permission to use the ADB logo.

Corrigenda to ADB publications may be found at http://www.adb.org/publications/corrigenda.

Note:
In this publication, "$" refers to United States dollars. ADB recognizes "Korea" as the Republic of Korea.

Cover photo by Christian Gallei.

Contents

Tables and boxes	iv
Acknowledgments	v
Abbreviations	vi
Glossary of terms	vii
Highlights	ix
Executive summary	x
Introduction	2
1 Setting the scene for a low-carbon and climate-resilient Asia and the Pacific	**3**
Global and regional context	3
ADB climate commitments and ambitions	4
Objectives of the ADB Climate Change Action Plan	6
2 How we operate: ADB's climate shift	**11**
Partnerships	11
Upscaling ADB climate investment and its impact	14
ADB's internal knowledge management and research	17
3 How we engage: ADB country engagement for climate action	**21**
Upstream: Strategic engagement for enhanced policy frameworks	22
Midstream: Embedding climate action in core institutions and national systems	25
Downstream: High-quality operations and implementation	28
4 How we deliver: Advancing low-carbon and climate-resilient solutions across operations	**31**
Integrated climate-smart planning and technology	31
Inclusive and climate-smart socioeconomic development	32
Climate-smart infrastructure	34
Biodiversity, agrifood systems, and nature-based climate solutions	36
Green and blue climate finance	38
5 Implementing and monitoring climate action	**45**
Appendixes	**48**
1 List of climate actions	49
2 Climate action by sector	60

Tables and boxes

TABLES

A2.1	Actions for low-carbon and climate-resilient agricultural development	63
A2.2	Actions for low-carbon and climate-resilient energy development	67
A2.3	Actions for low-carbon and climate-resilient finance development	72
A2.4	Actions for low-carbon and climate-resilient human and social development	75
A2.5	Actions for low-carbon and climate-resilient public sector management and governance development	80
A2.6	Actions for low-carbon and climate-resilient transport development	83
A2.7	Actions for low-carbon and climate-resilient water and urban development	88

BOXES

1	New financing models	12
2	Community Resilience Partnership Program	13
3	Leveraging finance and knowledge partnerships	14
4	ADF 13 Thematic Pool: Supporting disaster risk reduction and climate adaptation	15
5	ADB's Carbon Market Program	16
6	Differentiated approach for the Pacific	22
7	Enhancing climate change ambitions through nationally determined contributions	23
8	Regional climate action through Central Asia Regional Economic Cooperation	24
9	Regional multi-hazard climate and disaster risk assessments	24
10	Operationalizing Paris Agreement alignment in country programming processes	25
11	Enhancing climate action through domestic resource mobilization	26
12	Policy-based lending that drives climate action	27
13	Contingent disaster financing in the Pacific	27
14	Pakistan: Country Climate Investment Tracker and Visual Guide Dashboard	31
15	Integrated and holistic solutions to urban–rural development challenges	32
16	Bangladesh: Strengthening Social Resilience Program	33
17	Asia and the Pacific Water Resilience Initiative	34
18	Energy sector solutions	35
19	Examples of ADB initiatives on nature-based climate solutions	38
20	Example of support for climate and Sustainable Development Goal finance	39
21	Increasing leverage of national resources focused on climate investments	40
22	Shandong Green Development Fund Project	40
23	Action Plan for Healthy Oceans and Sustainable Blue Economies	41
24	Creating investable cities	41
25	Disaster relief or catastrophe bonds	42

Acknowledgments

The preparation of this Climate Change Action Plan (CCAP) was led by Alexandra Vogl together with Declan Magee and Fei Yu. The team benefited from the guidance of a core senior management team that included Bruno Carrasco, Toru Kubo, Noelle O'Brien, Vijay Padmanabhan, and Claus Astrup.

This CCAP could not have been prepared without the ownership and commitment of the working group, which included the following members from departments across the Asian Development Bank (ADB): Sabah Abdulla, Andrew J. Achimu, Tahmeen Ahmad, Bayarmaa Amarjargal, Dinesh Arora, Brigitte Balthasar, Fiona Bannert, Marina Rose Best, Sandeep Bhattacharya, Jeffrey Bowyer, Arup Kumar Chatterjee, Isabelle Chauche, Alexandra Pamela Chiang, Henry Young Choi, Jenny Yan Yee Chu, Andrew Clinton, Julia Cummins, Stefania Dina, Virender Kumar Duggal, Haidy Ear-Dupuy, Christian Ellermann, Alessio Giardino, Steven Goldfinch, Juan Francisco Gonzalez Jimenez, Sanjay Grover, Belinda Hewitt, Neil Hickey, Kate Hughes, Rika Idei, Anjum Israr, Narayan Iyer, Esmyra Javier, Okju Jeong, Stephanie Kamal, Thomas Kessler, Sarosh Khan, Ji Seon Kim, Sung Su Kim, Junkyu Lee, Malte Maass, Kirsteen Anne Mack, Paolo Manunta, Akira Matsunaga, Louise McSorley, David Morgado, Naeeda Crishna Morgado, Kee-Yung Nam, Mina Oh, Rabindra Osti, Wilhelmina Paz, Noel Peters, Aysha Qadir, Daniele Quaggiotto, Arun Ramamurthy, Brian Riley, Suzanne Kay Robertson, Delphine Roch, Susann Roth, Arghya Sinha Roy, Satomi Sakaguchi, Ruchika Saluja, Dustin Schinn, Aaron Sexton, Chaorin Shim, Hikaru Shoji, Lei Lei Song, Navin Twarakavi, Allison Woodruff, Zonibel Woods, Zheng Wu, and Jian Xu. The team is also grateful for the support provided by Amparo Dato, Tristan Knowles, Lindsay Marie Renaud, Young Seo, Guoliang Wu, and many other colleagues, especially those who supported working group members.

Country directors and resident missions provided invaluable feedback and were critical to enabling discussion with representatives from developing member countries.

High-level guidance and endorsement of actions was provided by the Climate Action Coordination Committee, chaired by Managing Director General Woochong Um. For CCAP preparation, the committee extended to a broader group of members that included Thomas Clark, Warren Evans, Suzanne Gaboury, Leah Gutierrez, Helen M. Hall, Stephanie K. C. Hung, F. Cleo Kawawaki, Muhammad Ehsan Khan, M. Teresa Kho, Tomoyuki Kimura, Lakshmi Menon, Stephen O'Leary, Albert F. Park, Ramesh Subramaniam, Aman K. Trana, Pierre N. Van Peteghem, John Versantvoort, Yasuto Watanabe, Winfried Wicklein, Bernard Leigh Woods, Kenichi Yokoyama, Yevgeniy Zhukov, and members of the CCAP core senior management team.

The CCAP team thanks the ADB Board of Directors for their guidance and direction, as well as representatives from developing member countries and civil society organizations for their feedback on previous drafts of the CCAP.

Strong support on coordination and administrative matters was provided by Janet Arlene Amponin, Arminda Meliz Bellen, Anna Liza Cinco, Ken Edward Concepcion, Ghia V. Rabanal, Nancy Bustamante, Bianca Gutierrez, and Mary Martha Merilo.

The team thanks Michael Lindfield for support along the way and the team of consultants involved in the critical initial CCAP development phase: Deborah Cornland, Xianfu Lu, Oesha Thakoerdin, John Ward, and Wei Zhou.

Peter Fredenburg edited the manuscript, and Rocilyn Laccay implemented typesetting and layout. The Department of Communications and Knowledge Management facilitated publication.

Abbreviations

ADB	Asian Development Bank
ADF	Asian Development Fund
ASEAN	Association of Southeast Asian Nations
CACC	Climate Action Coordination Committee
CCAP	Climate Change Action Plan
COP	Conference of the Parties of the UNFCCC
CRF	corporate results framework
CSO	civil society organization
DMC	developing member country
FCAS	fragile and conflict-affected situation
GHG	greenhouse gas
IPCC	Intergovernmental Panel on Climate Change
ISSB	International Sustainability Standards Board
MDB	multilateral development bank
MSME	micro, small, and medium-sized enterprise
NDC	nationally determined contribution
PPP	public–private partnership
SIDS	small island developing state
TA	technical assistance
UNFCCC	United Nations Framework Convention on Climate Change
WPBF	work program and budget framework

Glossary of terms

adaptation	Adjustment to actual or expected climate change and its effects that moderates harm or exploits beneficial opportunities.
blended finance	Concessional finance for the private sector operations of development finance institutions that combines concessional finance from donors or third parties with an institution's own account finance and/or commercial finance from other investors. It is used to develop private sector markets, address the Sustainable Development Goals, and mobilize private resources.
carbon market	Domestic or international platform for trading credits that represent measurable, reportable, and verifiable reductions in or the removal of GHG emissions.
carbon pricing	Approaches that internalize the cost of damage caused by climate change by putting a price on GHG emissions.
climate change	Long-term shifts in temperatures and weather patterns caused by either natural processes or human activities.
climate-resilient	The capacity to prepare for, respond to, and recover from the impacts of events caused by climate hazards with minimal damage to social well-being, the economy, and the environment.
climate-resilient pathway	Development trajectory that combines adaptation and mitigation in iterative, continually evolving processes to realize the goal of sustainable development.
climate-smart development	The integration of climate adaptation and mitigation measures into development planning, with the aim of achieving sustainable development while reducing GHG emissions and enhancing climate and disaster resilience.
differentiated approach	Addressing particular needs of DMCs, especially in SIDSs, FCASs, or mountainous regions in recognition of their vulnerability, fragility, and need to strengthen governance, institutions, and human capacity.
disaster	A serious disruption to the functioning of a community or society triggered by a geophysical hazard or extreme weather and entailing human, material, economic, and/or environmental losses.
energy transition	Structural change from a model of energy production and consumption based on fossil fuels to one that predominantly uses renewable and other low-carbon energy sources.
energy transition mechanism	A scalable, collaborative initiative that leverages a market-based approach to accelerate the transition from fossil fuels to clean energy.
extreme event	The occurrence of a value for a weather or climate variable above a defined threshold near the upper end of the range for that variable, or similarly below an opposing threshold.
greenhouse effect	Heat trapped close to the earth's surface by GHGs, such as carbon dioxide, methane, and nitrous oxide, thus making the earth warmer.

long-term climate strategy	A program of pathways by which a country aims to transition to low-carbon and climate-resilient development that is developed through intensive stakeholder dialogue led by that country, technical modeling, and analysis to guide sector transformation and investment plans for a net-zero future.
mitigation	Activities and efforts to reduce or limit GHG production or enhance GHG sequestration.
national adaptation plan	A country's effort to (i) reduce vulnerability to the impacts of climate change by building adaptive capacity and resilience, and (ii) integrate adaptation into new and existing national, sector, and subnational policies and programs, especially development strategies, plans, and budgets.
nationally determined contribution (NDC)	A nationally prepared plan by which a country outlines its efforts to reduce national GHG emissions and adapt to the impacts of climate change. NDCs are at the heart of the Paris Agreement and the achievement of its long-term goals. Article 4, paragraph 2 of the Paris Agreement requires each party to prepare, communicate, and maintain successive NDCs that it intends to achieve.
nature-based climate solution	A way to protect, better manage, and restore nature toward reducing GHG emissions, storing carbon, and enhancing climate resilience.
nature-based solution	An action to protect, conserve, restore, sustainably use, and manage natural or modified terrestrial, freshwater, coastal, and marine ecosystems in a way that addresses social, economic, and environmental challenges effectively and adaptively, while ensuring human well-being and resilience through ecosystem services and biodiversity benefits.
net zero	A state under which anthropogenic emissions of GHGs to the atmosphere are balanced by anthropogenic removals over a specified period.
Paris Agreement	A legally binding international treaty on climate change adopted by 196 parties at the United Nations Climate Change Conference in 2015. Its overarching goals are to hold the increase in the global average temperature to 1.5°C above pre-industrial levels, or certainly no more than 2.0°C, and to enhance climate resilience through adaptation to the unavoidable impacts of climate change.
sustainable public procurement	A purchasing and investment process that considers the economic, environmental, social, and institutional impacts of the entity's spending. It allows governments to meet their needs for goods, services, works, and utilities in a way that achieves value for money over the long term by generating benefits not only to the organization, but also to society and the economy, while remaining within the carrying capacity of the environment.
tipping point	A critical threshold in a climate system beyond which it reorganizes, often abruptly or irreversibly.
transformational change	Intervention that supports deep, systemic, and sustainable change and has potential for large-scale impact toward addressing climate change.

Highlights

The Asian Development Bank (ADB) has initiated a major reform to become the climate bank of Asia and the Pacific. The reform is matched with an increased ambition to provide $100 billion of its own funds, across public and private sector operations, to climate finance from 2019 to 2030. This will require ADB to develop a pipeline of high-quality climate projects and programs to support climate outcomes. Further, ADB has made ambitious commitments to align its sovereign and nonsovereign operations with the goals of the Paris Agreement. It will use its own funds to mobilize and enable climate investment by working with partners to achieve critical climate outcomes.

ADB will scale up its impact by catalyzing high-quality climate action through external finance. It is multiplying its own funds by raising additional climate finance from the private sector, philanthropies, capital markets, donors, and other sources. ADB is driving innovation in climate finance through cutting-edge initiatives such as the Innovative Finance Facility for Climate in Asia and the Pacific, the Energy Transition Mechanism, and the Climate Action Catalyst Fund, as well as innovative private sector projects. ADB partnerships with donors will continue to be key sources of concessional climate finance to support sovereign and private sector clients. These approaches have already raised considerable public and private finance for ADB developing member countries (DMCs). ADB will argue a strong case for higher grant and concessional finance for climate action in DMCs and continue to raise climate finance innovatively by exploring new partnerships and new ways to leverage and maximize the impact of partner funds.

ADB will continue to incentivize innovation in climate action with its own work and through partners to enhance its climate impact. From 2021 to 2023, ADB doubled its roster of climate technical experts to ensure that it has the skills needed to assist DMCs in their low-carbon and climate-resilient development. ADB will explore new ways to be more agile in responding to the needs of the public and private sector. Its activities will create an enabling environment and de-risk climate change and biodiversity investments by the private sector, partly by enabling reform to capital markets to promote greater financing for climate action. It will lead sector, thematic, and interdisciplinary innovation across the region, providing finance for new ideas, applying established and new technologies in its operations, and building partnerships that can tap innovation from the private sector and academia for climate impact. In building partnerships, ADB will develop thematic hubs able to leverage knowledge, adapt technology, and mobilize foreign direct investment and local resources to maximize climate impact.

ADB's new operating model enables it to work more effectively across regions, sectors, and themes to deliver multidisciplinary solutions to sovereign and private sector clients. At the country level, ADB will combine upstream policy and diagnostics to inform specific pathways and investments downstream. Country engagement will be reinforced by One ADB teams with interdisciplinary and complementary skill sets to ensure that ADB brings together the best technical, financial, operational, and knowledge solutions. Senior leadership on climate change across the organization will empower ADB to pursue climate action at scale and in a timely way, to mainstream climate analytics, and to mobilize the large amount of investment needed to support DMC efforts toward low-carbon and climate-resilient development.

Executive summary

A. Setting the scene for a low-carbon and climate-resilient Asia and the Pacific

After decades of steady progress in poverty reduction and socioeconomic development, humanity is at a crossroads. Climate change threatens to reverse development gains, deteriorate livelihoods, trigger displacement, and worsen poverty. Sustainable development and poverty reduction cannot be achieved without climate action. Asia and the Pacific are at the center of this challenge in terms of both the impact climate change will have on the lives of its people and the regional potential to combat climate change. As articulated in Strategy 2030, ADB is determined to play a lead role in helping the region pursue a path of low-carbon and climate-resilient development. Delivering the sustainable development outcomes envisioned in Strategy 2030 will require ADB to scale up its climate impact. This Climate Change Action Plan operationalizes ADB commitment and ambition to support the transition to a low-carbon and climate-resilient future in line with the Paris Agreement.

ADB goals to help its DMCs tackle climate change are ambitious. They include an ambition to provide $100 billion from its own resources—going beyond an earlier $80 billion commitment—for climate action by 2030, of which $34 billion will be for climate adaptation and resilience; multiplying ADB impact by catalyzing large sums of public and private climate finance; and aligning ADB sovereign and nonsovereign operations with the mitigation and adaptation goals of the Paris Agreement. The action plan proposes how ADB will deliver on these commitments and ambitions and what changes it will make to drive climate action in the region. ADB will follow several principles and drivers: (i) being client-centric, (ii) creating a bottom-up and iterative process to develop and refine actions, (iii) prioritizing programmatic approaches for transformational impact, (iv) setting private sector mobilization as an important cornerstone of climate efforts, (v) pursuing evidence-based approaches and innovation, (vi) promoting integrated and multisector solutions, and (vii) supporting a just transition in its DMCs that distributes the costs and benefits of climate action fairly. The action plan fully aligns with ADB's new operating model and its four shifts to enhance ADB's role as the climate bank for Asia and the Pacific; increase support for private sector development; deliver innovative, knowledge-driven, and integrated solutions; and modernize ADB ways of working.

B. How we operate: ADB's climate shift

To multiply its climate impact, ADB will leverage partnerships that generate and deliver finance and knowledge. It will work with diverse partners to explore new financing models that expand lending capacity and leverage resources for climate finance. Examples include the Innovative Finance Facility for Climate in Asia and the Pacific, Energy Transition Mechanism, Climate Action Catalyst Fund, and Community Resilience Partnership Program, as well as innovative private sector projects funded by ADB directly or by mobilizing other funds. ADB will deepen its knowledge partnerships, regional partnerships for regional public goods, and engagement with civil society organizations. ADB will closely follow the evolving financial architecture on loss and damage and is committed to playing its part to support the most vulnerable communities' efforts to minimize and address loss and damage.

ADB will boost investment impact through a programmatic approach that mainstreams climate in its operations. This features more use of programmatic financing modalities such as policy-based and results-based lending, as well as sector development programs, to create an enabling environment for greater climate investment, especially from the private sector. The approach will complement and expand opportunities for sector-wide projects that align with the Paris Agreement and a transition to a low-carbon economy. To maximize the climate impact of its deployed capital, ADB will assess possibilities to establish a categorization system for operations with highly beneficial climate impacts that will include new incentives for higher contributions to climate outcomes. ADB will be strategic in its use of technical assistance (TA) to ensure that it drives transformational change.

ADB will increase its own investment in climate finance and expand its efforts to catalyze other public and private investment. It will work with donors to dedicate additional concessional resources to global and regional public goods, including for climate change, in the 14th replenishment of the Asian Development Fund. Through a recent update of its Capital Adequacy Framework, ADB approved capital management reform that unlocks $100 billion in new funding capacity over the next decade to respond to evolving challenges in the region, including climate change. ADB will explore more concessional terms for climate projects and pilot new financing structures and instruments. ADB will build on its efforts to enable DMC access to concessional finance from Climate Investment Funds, the Green Climate Fund, and other multilateral and bilateral sources. Partnerships for concessional climate finance that blend private and public investment have been, and will continue to be, instrumental to a rapid transition to a low-carbon economy in Asia and the Pacific.

ADB will employ a holistic approach to mobilizing private capital. It will promote public and private capital deployment through transaction advisory services and help DMCs reform legal and regulatory frameworks to attract private investment. ADB will align its activities in the private sector and in public–private partnership with its climate ambitions. It will maximize opportunities for mobilizing carbon finance to make more financially attractive public and private investment in low-carbon technologies and business models. ADB will complement its continued provision of loan instruments with other instruments, notably guarantees, risk participation, and equity. It will scale up blended finance for climate action in coordination with partners and in line with blended finance principles agreed by multilateral development banks.

ADB will enhance access to global climate knowledge. This includes more digital literacy for knowledge sharing and linking climate change knowledge across operations. Through regional cooperation, ADB will build coalitions to address the regional climate agenda and deepen engagement with civil society organizations to drive climate action.

C. How we engage: ADB country engagement for climate action

ADB will offer countries comprehensive climate solutions upstream, midstream, and downstream. A fully integrated package of climate solutions that tap sovereign and private sector expertise will explore differentiated approaches for DMCs—especially for fragile and conflict-affected situations, small island developing states, and mountainous countries, in recognition of their particular climate change needs. Complementary to country-level engagement, ADB will engage international partners and investors, particularly in regional and thematic hubs, to channel more international climate finance into DMCs.

Upstream, ADB will enhance policy frameworks for climate change. It will integrate climate change more deeply into its country partnership and regional strategies. ADB will coordinate with multiple donors on the use of country development platforms for climate action, and thus ensure long-term programming horizons. It will help DMCs optimize and realize their climate ambitions through nationally determined contributions, long-term strategies, and national adaptation plans. It will support a just transition, recognizing that climate change affects women and men differently. ADB will continue to use its regional mandate to help DMCs meet regional climate challenges by providing TA for regional solutions, building regional platforms for enhanced project design and financing, supporting regional action on climate change, and promoting international trade and investment oriented toward climate solutions.

Midstream, ADB will help DMCs integrate climate action into national plans and budgets. It will work with them on climate-responsive public finance management, especially to strengthen links between climate planning and budget processes and procurement systems. ADB will provide support for strong coherence and integration between climate plans and sector policies, plans, road maps, investment frameworks, projects, and programs. It will work with other development partners to include low-carbon and climate-resilient considerations in guidance on public investment management, public expenditure and financial accountability, and other fiscal toolkits. It will support private sector decarbonization and climate-resilient corporate road maps.

Downstream, projects and programs must be high quality to reap the full benefits of enhanced climate policies. Enhanced project diagnostics and preparation are key to strong operational support for climate outcomes. Through transaction advisory TA, ADB will continue to support the preparation and delivery of climate-resilient infrastructure. It will further improve its guidelines for high-quality climate projects and enhance safeguards to better manage climate risks. It will work with clients to develop comprehensive project financing plans and incorporate better risk assessment. Sustainable procurement will be promoted for individual projects and at the country level. ADB will continue to provide implementation support and capacity building to ensure the successful delivery of climate investments.

ADB will engage strategically with the private sector regionally and in individual DMCs. It will engage with the private sector to understand the opportunities and challenges that climate change poses to companies. Through private sector assessments, country partnership strategies, ongoing client relationship management, and climate opportunity mapping in DMCs and regional hubs, ADB private sector operations will build on existing relationships and develop new ones across target sectors—notably infrastructure, agribusiness, social and health, manufacturing, real estate, and financial intermediation—to increase private sector support through direct assistance and through midstream and upstream reform.

D. How we deliver: Advancing low-carbon and climate-resilient solutions across operations

ADB will integrate climate-smart planning and technology with holistic approaches to combat climate change and enhance climate and disaster resilience. It will use whole-of-economy and whole-of-society planning approaches to climate mitigation and adaptation, and to disaster risk reduction. ADB can leverage its multisector expertise to design and implement comprehensive planning approaches that encompass effective low-carbon and risk-reduction planning at the subnational, national, and regional level. It will work with national and subnational governments to strengthen ties between climate and sector objectives in the planning process, notably functional linkages between urban and rural areas. ADB will promote technological progress at early planning and design stages with investment in technological adaptation, piloting, testing, and demonstration.

Climate change places a major strain on socioeconomic development in Asia and the Pacific. It is critical to scale up support for strengthened resilience, including in service delivery to meet the needs of women, poor and vulnerable populations, people with disabilities, the elderly, and young people. Climate change is a critical risk to improving human health outcomes. In the same way, climate action must be embedded in education systems by developing low-carbon education infrastructure and ensuring that systems support the development of skills necessary for a low-carbon and climate-resilient transition. ADB will complement this by investing in climate-adaptive and shock-responsive social protection, thereby ensuring that social protection programs are informed by appropriate national and regional adaptation and disaster-risk management. Building climate awareness at a young age will be pursued through assistance with curriculum development in primary schools.

Energy, transport, and urban infrastructure are major and rising sources of greenhouse gas (GHG) emissions. Such investments must be made more low carbon and climate resilient, with the energy sector playing a critical role in decarbonization. ADB will facilitate a transition to sustainable, lower-carbon, and resilient energy systems by deploying renewable energy and accelerating improved energy efficiency across power, heating, and cooling systems, as well as other energy-intensive industries and buildings. Urgent action is required to reduce emissions from transport, which is the fastest-growing source of carbon emissions globally. ADB will support the decarbonization of transport in Asia and the Pacific through an avoid–shift–improve approach that favors low-carbon multimodal transport systems, including electric-powered mobility, and through support for transport systems that are climate resilient.

ADB will mainstream biodiversity in its operations toward a nature-positive portfolio. Biodiversity loss is a key driver of climate change, creating an urgent need to halt negative impacts. Nature sequesters carbon effectively and provides other services for climate mitigation and adaptation. The region has high potential for employing cost-effective nature-based solutions for low-carbon and climate-resilient development. ADB will study and develop nature-based climate solutions, recognizing that carbon finance can extend incentives to nature-based climate solutions.

Agrifood systems need urgent transformation to meet both climate objectives and food security needs. Agrifood systems contribute almost a third of global GHG emissions, and feeding a growing population with diverse food and nutrition needs entails risks of even higher GHG emissions. Meanwhile, agrifood systems in Asia and the Pacific are dominated by smallholder farmers who are among the people most vulnerable to climate change. To achieve the climate transition in agrifood systems, investment needs to be scaled up. Future ADB investment in agriculture, food, and nature will be climate-smart, proactively pursuing opportunities for GHG reduction and climate mitigation and adaptation while ensuring high productivity and a just transition. It will focus primarily on high-impact links in agribusiness value chains, irrigation and water resource management, and nature-based climate solutions.

The private sector will be supported to align financial flows with the transition to net-zero and climate-resilient development. Through private sector interventions, ADB will help corporations and others in the private sector align financial flows with net-zero and climate-resilient development through long-term partnerships and investment across target sectors, notably infrastructure, agribusiness, social, manufacturing, real estate, and financial intermediation. Direct and indirect investment will channel ADB's own financing and cofinancing to firms and individuals in the private sector.

ADB will support green and blue climate finance to ensure that investments have positive environmental, climate, and social impacts. ADB will partner with central banks, the private sector and others on setting standards to build sustainable capital markets that align with the Paris Agreement and accelerate green finance with innovative mechanisms able to close a large climate financing gap. ADB will work with DMCs to expand traditional sources of green climate finance, strengthen public financial and investment management systems, review fossil fuel subsidies, and explore opportunities in international carbon markets.

E. Implementing and monitoring climate action

The Climate Change Action Plan (CCAP) has implications for everyone in ADB. As an organization, ADB must walk the talk by shrinking its own carbon footprint and by ensuring that each part of ADB is working out how it can drive climate action. ADB has more than doubled its number of climate staff since 2021 and will continue to deepen its climate expertise through recruitment and incentives for all staff, including training on climate change. ADB has developed guidance for staff to address climate in operations and will continue to do so.

ADB will embed the CCAP into its key corporate processes. It will continue to use key performance indicators on climate in its corporate results framework. Climate action will be integrated into the ADB work program and budget framework, which will be reviewed as actions are adjusted and added.

Actions listed in the CCAP will be regularly updated to ensure quality and relevance. Proposed actions in Appendixes 1 and 2 will be monitored regularly and may be updated or revised as and when needed. It is proposed that the CCAP be revisited in a midterm review in 2026, and it will undergo a final review in 2030. The Climate Change and Disaster Risk Management Advisory Group will coordinate the implementation of proposed actions and report progress to the Climate Action Coordination Committee, which will oversee CCAP implementation.

Introduction

To guide accelerated action by the Asian Development Bank (ADB) on climate change, this Climate Change Action Plan, 2023–2030 (CCAP) outlines ADB's commitment to strategic interventions and initiatives to spearhead climate action. The CCAP aims to direct ADB's strategic vision and policies—including Strategy 2030 and key shifts in ADB's new operating model—to ensure high-quality climate outcomes.

Considering developments in international climate and development policy processes, as well as internal analyses,[1] the CCAP follows a One ADB approach, developed through extensive consultation with ADB staff, Management, and the Board of Directors, and in discussions with ADB members and civil society organizations. With the CCAP, ADB supports transformational change within the institution and across Asia and the Pacific.

Interventions and initiatives proposed under the CCAP are meant to ensure high-quality and far-reaching positive climate outcomes, continued innovation on climate action, and future expansion of climate ambitions and targets. The CCAP is a living document that will allow ADB to learn from its own work and the work of others and to update, from time to time, its proposed interventions and initiatives (Appendix 1: List of climate actions and Appendix 2: Climate action by sector). This will give ADB flexibility to respond to realities on the ground and ensure that its climate work remains high-quality and relevant.

---

[1] In particular, the CCAP considers findings in an evaluation report by ADB's Independent Evaluation Department and the ongoing midterm review of Strategy 2030 and its operational priorities. IED. 2021. *ADB Support for Action on Climate Change, 2011–2020*.

1 Setting the scene for a low-carbon and climate-resilient Asia and the Pacific

1.1 Global and regional context

Global progress in poverty reduction and socioeconomic development is at risk. In recent decades, significant progress has been made in poverty reduction and socioeconomic development. Despite this, many challenges remain, and the outbreak of coronavirus disease (COVID-19) was a stark reminder of how quickly progress can be reversed. The impacts of climate change are becoming pronounced: more intense and frequent extreme weather but also slow-onset impacts such as sea-level rise and unseasonal weather. Climate change is hindering development, exacerbating inequality, potentially worsening poverty, and putting hundreds of millions of lives at risk. The threat it poses is real and, without concerted action, will only worsen.

The world is at a development crossroads. Sustainable development promises green growth and improved livelihoods, while business as usual threatens great destruction. Despite significant efforts to address climate change in recent years, gains still fall short of what is required. The Intergovernmental Panel on Climate Change (IPCC) warns of a rapidly closing window of opportunity to secure a livable and sustainable future for all, as warming will likely exceed 1.5°C by the 2030s and 3.2°C by the end of the century. This would irreversibly worsen multiple climate hazards and present multiple risks to ecosystems and humans. The IPCC is clear that loss and damage will hit the most vulnerable people and ecosystems hardest, highlighting the importance of a just transition to development that is climate resilient and sustainable.[2] The IPCC report notes the perils of breaching tipping points and the high cost of failure to act in time.

Asia and the Pacific are on the frontline of the climate crisis. The region is home to more than half of the world's population, 17 of 36 global biodiversity hotspots, many of the world's fastest-growing economies, and six economies that are among the top global carbon emitters. It contributes more than half of all greenhouse gas (GHG) emissions. The region is also highly vulnerable to extreme weather and related disasters, with annual losses estimated at $675 billion and disproportionate impacts on women, poor and vulnerable populations, people with disabilities, the elderly, and young people. Many people in ADB developing member countries (DMCs) are highly exposed and vulnerable to climate change impacts, living in low-lying small island developing states (SIDSs) like those in the Pacific; in fragile and conflict-affected situations (FCASs), notably around the disappearing Aral Sea; and downstream of the Himalayan and Tianshan mountain ranges. ADB recognizes that the climate crisis is tied to other global environmental challenges such as rapid biodiversity loss, air and soil pollution, and runaway urbanization. The resulting "polycrisis" requires a holistic approach, not isolated fixes.

Climate action is falling short in Asia and the Pacific. Current nationally determined contribution (NDC) commitments and GHG trajectories are projected to bring a 16% increase in emissions in Asia and the Pacific from 2010 to 2030.[3] While plans to adapt have progressed, interventions are generally small, fragmented, and incremental, as large financing gaps hinder the implementation of enhanced climate action. DMCs need to integrate their development pathways with low-carbon and climate-resilient transformations that can sustainably lift millions of people out of poverty.

DMCs need significantly more climate finance to address climate change and enhance climate resilience. To ease the climate crisis, it is essential to shift to low-carbon and climate-resilient development pathways. Achieving

---

[2] IPCC. 2023. *AR6 Synthesis Report: Climate Change 2023*.
[3] Economic and Social Commission for Asia and the Pacific. 2022. *Review of Climate Ambition in Asia and the Pacific: Raising NDC Targets with Enhanced Nature-Based Solutions*.

this transformation requires substantial investment and innovation.[4] Countries in Asia and the Pacific need significant financing and support to meet their NDC targets and set higher ambitions in subsequent NDCs. This requires them to mobilize both external climate finance and domestic resources for climate action. FCASs face further constraints and need more targeted support and funding modalities. Huge investments are required to meet the goals of the Paris Agreement and support the shift to net-zero development pathways. Significant sums of climate finance are required as well to meet adaptation needs in Asia and the Pacific.

Innovative approaches that accelerate private and public investment are necessary to address climate change. Estimates show that $7.1 trillion in new benefits could accrue from investing $1.8 trillion globally from 2020 to 2030 in five areas of climate adaptation: early warning systems, resilient infrastructure, dryland crop production, protecting mangroves, and managing water resources for resilience.[5] Climate action provides new business prospects for the private sector, and international carbon markets can attract innovative carbon finance to incentivize and catalyze investments in low-carbon technologies and solutions.[6]

1.2 ADB climate commitments and ambitions

Strategy 2030 charts how ADB can help Asia and the Pacific meet its changing needs. Under Strategy 2030, ADB has sustained efforts to eradicate extreme poverty and expand its vision of a prosperous, inclusive, resilient, and sustainable Asia and the Pacific.[7] Strategy 2030 recognizes significant diversity in DMCs and prioritizes support for the poorest and most vulnerable among them. ADB's Corporate Results Framework, 2019–2024 (CRF) aligns with Strategy 2030 to assess development progress in Asia and the Pacific and how effectively ADB delivers development results.[8] Since Strategy 2030 and the CRF were approved, ADB has redoubled its commitment to addressing climate change and becoming the climate bank of Asia and the Pacific.

Operational Priority 3 of Strategy 2030 is a central avenue for climate objectives. Aiming to scale up support for addressing climate change, disaster risks, and environmental degradation, Operational Priority 3 seeks to grow the portfolio of ADB climate projects and investments and improve their quality. A current midterm review of Strategy 2030 cites the need to enhance upstream engagement, expand private sector operations, and strengthen staff skills. ADB must complement this with further diversification of its portfolio and financing modalities, increased use of transformational approaches to climate adaptation and resilience, and more collaboration with DMCs as they implement their climate policies and strategies. ADB has already developed forward-looking sector directional guides that assess the main sector challenges posed by climate change and other developments.[9]

Climate change is a critical factor for each operational priority under Strategy 2030. Making progress on Operational Priority 2 (Accelerating progress in gender equality) requires understanding the disproportionate impact of climate change on women and girls and that climate action must be designed with this in mind. Supporting women's economic empowerment and gender equality in decision-making and leadership requires that gender equality be mainstreamed in climate action. Operational Priorities 4 (Making cities more livable) and 5 (Promoting rural development and food security) are deeply intertwined with climate change and disaster risk management, as sustained progress is impossible without climate action. Operational Priority 6 (Strengthening governance and institutional capacity) is at the core of the midstream approach discussed in section 3 below. The transboundary nature of climate change and its impact renders critical the interplay between climate action and Operational Priority 7 (Fostering regional cooperation and integration).

---

[4] To achieve net zero, Asia and the Pacific will need to spend an estimated $3.1 trillion annually on physical energy and transport assets, or half again more than current spending. McKinsey. 2022. *Asia's Net-Zero Transition: Opportunity and Risk amid Climate Action*.
[5] Global Center on Adaptation. 2019. *Adapt Now: A Global Call for Leadership on Climate Resilience*.
[6] ADB. 2018. *Decoding Article 6 of the Paris Agreement*.
[7] ADB. 2018. *Strategy 2030: Achieving a Prosperous, Inclusive, Resilient, and Sustainable Asia and the Pacific*.
[8] ADB. 2019. *Corporate Results Framework, 2019–2024: Policy Paper*.
[9] Strategy 2030 directional guides are developed for the following sectors: education, energy, finance, health, transport, and urban and water. Details are available at https://www.adb.org/who-we-are/about/sector-directional-guides.

A range of ADB policies, plans, and frameworks steer operations relevant to climate. Aside from Strategy 2030 and its operational priorities, ADB includes climate considerations across the full spectrum of its work.[10] In 2021, for example, ADB adopted a new energy policy that says no to coal and includes moving from conventional carbon-intensive power systems to low- and zero-carbon systems, partly through the use of digital technology to integrate variable renewable energy sources.[11] Energy policy implementation is supported by guidance notes on natural gas operations, waste-to-energy projects, and large hydropower projects.

ADB has identified several climate commitments and ambitions:

(i) aligning with the mitigation and adaptation goals of the Paris Agreement for 100% of sovereign operations and 85% of nonsovereign operation finance since July 2023, and 100% of nonsovereign operations finance by July 2025;[12]
(ii) raising $80 billion in climate finance from its own resources in 2019–2030, toward a total ambition of $100 billion, with cumulative mitigation finance expected to reach $66 billion and cumulative adaptation finance expected to reach $34 billion;[13]
(iii) reaching $9 billion in climate adaptation finance in 2019–2024;[14]
(iv) supporting private initiatives with $12 billion of the $100 billion in cumulative climate finance from own resources in 2019–2030 and aiming to crowd in another $18 billion–$30 billion;[15] and
(v) ensuring that at least 65% of its operations support climate change mitigation and/or adaptation by 2024, and 75% by 2030, as assessed using a 3-year rolling average.

ADB is transforming itself to better facilitate DMC delivery of climate action. Four interconnected shifts in ADB's new operating model allow ADB to (i) enhance its position as the climate bank for Asia and the Pacific; (ii) increase support for private sector development; (iii) deliver innovative, knowledge-driven, and integrated solutions; and (iv) modernize its ways of working. ADB resident missions will act as one-stop shops for all ADB operations, both sovereign and nonsovereign. To serve DMCs, bank-wide One ADB teams, led by resident missions, will be staffed with sector, thematic, private sector, market development, fiduciary system, and public–private partnership (PPP) specialists.[16] This will enable greater specialization, agility, and collaboration; reduce expertise fragmentation and thereby enhance synergy; place expertise closer to clients; offer integrated solutions to better address intersectionality across sectors; and translate innovation and operational experiences quickly into reusable and actionable knowledge for clients.

The international community has called on ADB and other multilateral development banks (MDBs) to step up their climate ambitions. The call—which comes from ADB members, other stakeholders including civil society, the Conference of the Parties of the United Nations Framework Convention on Climate Change (UNFCCC), and notably the Group of Twenty in the *G20 New Delhi Leaders' Declaration*—is a vote of confidence in ADB's commitment to low-carbon and climate-resilient development and encouragement for ADB to be even bolder in supporting DMC efforts to transition to low-carbon and climate-resilient economies.

---

[10] Prior to publishing Strategy 2030, ADB published the Climate Change Operational Framework, 2017–2030, which broadly directs how to strengthen climate action and enhance resilience.
[11] ADB. 2021. *2021 Energy Policy of the Asian Development Bank: Supporting Low-Carbon Transition in Asia and the Pacific*.
[12] As a multilateral development bank (MDB), ADB follows the Joint MDB Alignment Approach to the Paris Agreement, of which ADB is a signatory, and the common MDB assessment methodologies developed as part of that framework.
[13] In 2019–2022, actual cumulative climate finance commitments from ADB resources amounted to $21 billion. Refined climate finance projections by region and sector will be developed in 2024, reflecting the $100 billion climate finance ambition for 2019–2030.
[14] Accounting follows the MDB *Joint Methodology for Tracking Climate Change Adaptation Finance* published in 2022.
[15] ADB. 2021. *ADB Raises 2019–2030 Climate Finance Ambition to $100 Billion*. News release. 13 October.
[16] ADB. 2022. *Organizational Review: A New Operating Model to Accelerate ADB's Transformation toward Strategy 2030 and Beyond*.

1.3 Objectives of the ADB Climate Change Action Plan

ADB will do its part toward sustainable development and a low-carbon and climate-resilient transition in Asia and the Pacific. ADB has played a critical role supporting DMCs' sustainable, resilient, and inclusive development. The CCAP lays out enhanced action to achieve ADB's commitments and ambitions and proposes actions to help DMCs move more strongly toward a low-carbon and climate-resilient trajectory. It highlights priorities for accelerated climate action through financial, technical, and knowledge support, and through regional and private sector initiatives. By implementing the CCAP, ADB will help Asia and the Pacific develop in a manner that contributes to the Sustainable Development Goals and aligns with the goals of the Paris Agreement and the Sendai Framework on Disaster Risk Reduction.[17]

Constraints inhibit ADB facilitation of low-carbon and climate-resilient development in Asia and the Pacific. While ADB must commit its own financial resources including concessional finance, it must also collaborate with other finance institutions. Limits on ADB financial resources may constrain its convening power and effective engagement in policy dialogue with DMCs, weakening its ability to shape regional public opinion and engage the private sector. Key constraints on DMCs are (i) low awareness of the consequences of inaction on climate change and the cost of deferral, (ii) limited access to capital markets and especially concessional resources, (iii) insufficient absorptive capacity to take on more investments, and (iv) poor access to affordable technologies with which to transition to low-carbon and resilient economies.

ADB can enhance its climate action and impact through interventions in several areas. Addressing key constraints and promoting more climate-focused use of ADB resources will boost the scale and quality of investments that offer low-carbon and climate-resilient outcomes. The CCAP identifies as key interventions (i) internal reforms to maximize climate investments, enable partnerships, and strengthen knowledge management; (ii) stronger strategic and programmatic approaches for engagement with clients; and (iii) the delivery of low-carbon and climate-resilient solutions at a scale sufficient to have meaningful climate outcomes. Climate actions are designed to achieve targets set out in Strategy 2030 and the CRF, realize the ADB climate ambition, and set the tone and pace for activity beyond 2030.

The CCAP is guided by principles and drivers to ensure a low-carbon and climate-resilient trajectory in a just, effective, and efficient manner:

(i) **Client-centric: Put the climate-related needs of DMCs and their people at the heart of ADB support.** Recognizing the importance of country ownership and coordination with in-country efforts, including those of development partners, ADB will tailor its support to respect and reflect how each DMC differs in terms of its priorities and climate challenges. ADB support will comprehensively include policy development, transaction advisory and project selection services, project financing, corporate and finance sector financing, and capacity strengthening. It will be informed by in-depth understanding of institutional, physical, socioeconomic, and political opportunities and constraints on climate action. ADB interventions will strengthen community and institutional resilience. At a national level, ADB interventions will help implement and update NDCs, long-term climate strategies, national adaptation plans, and other climate policies and action plans, integrating climate considerations into planning and budgeting processes to support climate action alongside economic growth.

(ii) **Bottom-up and iterative: Enable a process that allows ADB to adapt actions to reflect good practices and realities on the ground.** Climate change is a constantly moving target as understanding of its impact evolves with new scientific discoveries. The CCAP must create a dynamic process that allows ADB to refine and adjust its approach and actions to reflect the latest evidence, good practices, and lessons learned from its efforts and those of its partners, and that responds appropriately to change in the nature of the climate challenge confronting each DMC. Climate action needs to be determined using a bottom-up approach together with those closest to the problem. Program co-creation and co-design better ensure meaningful outcomes that are sustained over the long term.

---

[17] United Nations Office for Disaster Risk Reduction. 2015. *Sendai Framework on Disaster Risk Reduction 2015–2030*.

(iii) **High impact: Prioritize approaches for transformational interventions with requisite scale and speed.** In line with MDB common principles and methodologies on climate change, actions will be prioritized to pursue rapid and scalable mitigation and adaptation impacts, such as through the accelerated retirement or repurposing of large plants powered by coal and other fossil fuels, the decarbonization of transport and energy-intensive industries, and a just transition for agriculture and other land uses. Private sector mobilization will be critical for success. Other priority actions will build resilience in coastal and other highly vulnerable populations through integrated support that addresses infrastructure, ecosystems, livelihoods, and institutional development, and will shape market demand by focusing procurement requirements more firmly on sustainability. In fragile operating environments, innovative approaches that reduce vulnerability to climate impacts will be piloted first to build trust with local partners and stakeholders and better incorporate local and contextual knowledge in programs, and only then scaled up.

(iv) **Private sector participation: Prioritize policy reform and action that encourage the private sector to deliver climate solutions and innovations.** ADB will mobilize private finance at scale in targeted sectors through instruments and structures that minimize risk posed to private partners' trade and investment pipelines. Enhanced action will engage the private sector to fill financing gaps and develop, deploy, and apply climate adaptation at scale, and to foster mitigation by private equity funds and finance institutions. Proven mechanisms in the ADB toolkit that leverage private sector capacity and engagement in financing international trade will be aligned with climate priorities. Interventions will support national climate policies, regulatory frameworks including market-based instruments that prompt behavioral change, bankable project development and deal structuring, and innovative financing solutions that minimize investment risk and create incentives for the private sector to engage. ADB will work directly with subnational entities—municipalities, provinces, and state-owned enterprises—to strengthen their resilience and creditworthiness and to leverage private climate finance through green bonds, commercial lending, and PPP. It will continue to mobilize grant resources to incentivize and de-risk private sector investment in climate action.

(v) **Evidence-based: Ensure that ADB climate action is founded on practical experience and data and includes forward-looking, innovative approaches.** By building on knowledge drawn from partnerships with academia, industry, civil society, and vulnerable and indigenous people, ADB will ensure that climate action builds on existing know-how and data. Ensuring that climate decisions and action are evidence-based and robust requires ADB and DMCs to have capacity to seek out and exploit the latest science and knowledge: climate data, climate-modeling tools, and related spatial information and technology. Special consideration will apply in FCAS, SIDS, and other situations where information is hard to come by, to ensure that information shortfalls do not stifle action.

(vi) **Integrated solutions: Prioritize systemic, resource-efficient, and multisector solutions in close collaboration with partners.** Priorities will be integrated solutions that simultaneously address financial, knowledge, and institutional challenges, and multisector interventions that maximize synergy between mitigation and adaptation and among partners. ADB recognizes that climate change and the drivers of environmental degradation and biodiversity loss are inextricably linked, and that promoting resilience requires well-functioning and diverse ecosystems, with nature playing a crucial role in storing carbon and avoiding GHG emissions. Integrated solutions that address these linkages will be pursued toward sustainable urban, food, agriculture, and forestry development; human and animal health; and land-use and marine management. In addition, ADB will further leverage the commonality of actions and partnerships to enhance climate and disaster resilience and will emphasize disaster risk reduction as a key entry point for strengthening resilience.

(vii) **Just transition: Create a low-carbon and climate-resilient future with new economic and social development opportunities that leave no one behind.** ADB commitment for a just transition aims to deliver climate objectives while enabling socioeconomic benefits, thus accelerating progress toward both the Paris Agreement and the Sustainable Development Goals. ADB support for a just transition aligns with agreed principles for MDB support.[18] It recognizes a multifaceted lens for a just transition as it applies across workers, communities, consumers, and producers. ADB support for a just transition recognizes that processes, like outcomes, must be people-centric and just. Genuinely inclusive, transparent, and accountable processes are central to successful support for a just transition. Challenges and opportunities associated with a just transition are context-specific, reflecting the place and people affected, and thus require local, regional, and national engagement and ownership. It is therefore important that support for a just transition be developed and delivered in consultation with affected groups, including civil society, women, workers' associations, trade unions, and marginalized populations.

---

[18] ADB. 2021. *ADB Joins MDBs to Support Just Transition toward Net-Zero Economies*. News release. 29 October.

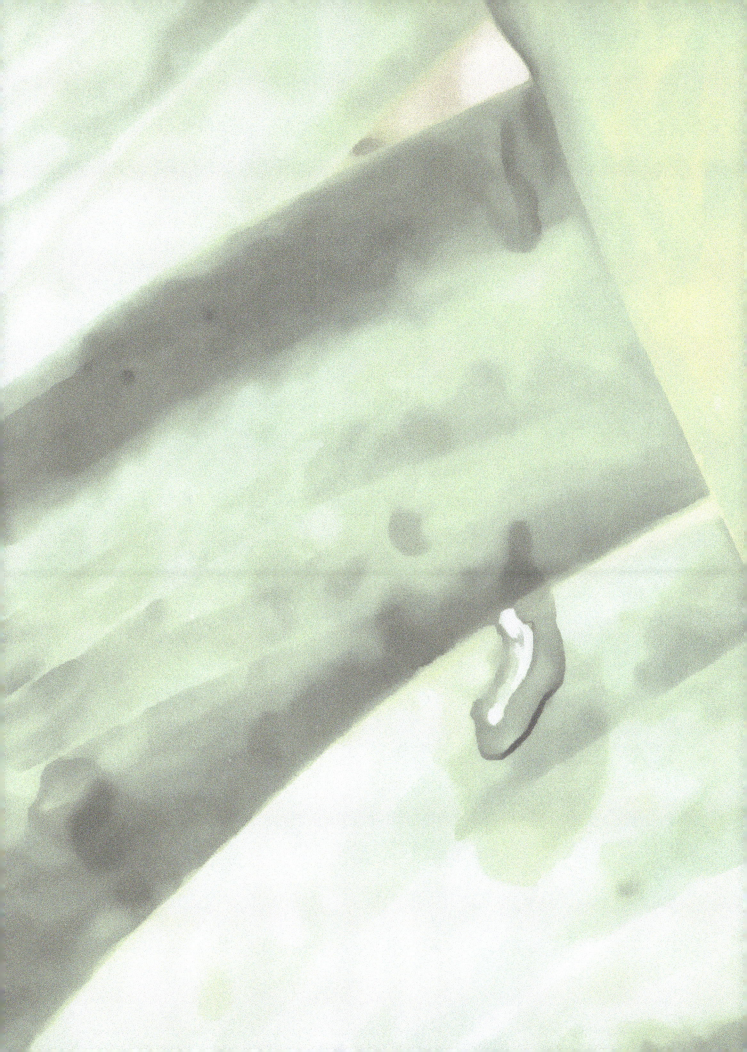

2 How we operate: ADB's climate shift

ADB will combine partnerships, innovative finance, and knowledge that help DMCs scale up their climate actions. It will build diverse partnerships and coordinate resource mobilization to pool financial resources, share risks, and combine knowledge and technical expertise toward planning and implementing climate-informed development programs and projects. ADB's role as the regional climate bank will depend on its scaling up climate finance and impact. By proactively generating new evidence and knowledge, ADB will help DMCs improve their climate policies and programs toward generating private sector investment opportunities and enabling an environment for investment.

2.1 Partnerships

Climate action needs much more investment than any single actor can deliver. According to the United Nations Framework Convention on Climate Change (UNFCCC), cumulative financing needs in Asia and the Pacific will come to $11.8 trillion by 2030, with $3.8 trillion earmarked for adaptation.[19] Global climate finance mobilization to date falls far short of these estimates. The public and private sector alike need to scale up climate investment significantly. The whole finance sector requires fundamental reorientation, which provides scope for ADB to strengthen its role as a convener and facilitator of multiple forms of partnership for stronger climate outcomes.

ADB will enhance and deepen current partnerships. Partners include (i) international finance institutions and development assistance agencies; (ii) dedicated climate funds, in particular the Green Climate Fund, Global Environment Facility, and Climate Investment Funds; (iii) national and subnational governments and agencies; (iv) international and national private sectors; (v) public and private risk-mitigation institutions such as insurance companies and guarantee entities; and (vi) philanthropies. ADB is committed to strengthening climate outcomes by fostering close and regular collaboration and engagement among partners for comprehensive in-country consultation. ADB will thus support country climate development platforms to improve partner coordination in developing climate finance solutions at scale and consolidate climate partnership structures that ensure cohesive and consistent approaches to engagement with development partners. Coordination and collaboration with other MDBs are particularly important to ensure synergy.

ADB explores new financing models to expand its lending capacity and leverage resources for climate finance. ADB will redouble its efforts to provide access to grants and concessional finance for DMCs while continuing to meet the needs of the poorest countries. Existing channels of concessional financing will be expanded, and new channels created, to incentivize investment in global and regional public goods addressing climate change. ADB will enhance its efforts to channel partners' grants and loans earmarked for financing climate projects into its existing vehicles for project-specific cofinancing, trust funds, and other special funds. It will explore new models for financing partnerships and platforms, including philanthropic vehicles for blended finance, and new finance tools, engaging with a broader range of partners to better leverage scarce resources. Examples of new financing models are the Innovative Finance Facility for Climate in Asia and the Pacific, Energy Transition Mechanism, ASEAN Catalytic Green Finance Facility of the Association of Southeast Asian Nations, and Climate Action Catalyst Fund (Box 1). ADB will make greater use of credit-enhancing instruments, especially guarantees to leverage financing from partners. It is exploring how large debt conversions could be used as debt-for-nature swaps, while ramping up partnership with commercial banks to provide for low-carbon development through finance intermediaries.

---

[19] UNFCCC. Standing Committee on Finance. 2021. *Determination of the Needs of Developing Country Parties*. The report includes East and South Asian DMCs, not all of which include adaptation in their NDCs.

> **Box 1: New financing models**
>
> **Innovative Finance Facility for Climate in Asia and the Pacific.** IF-CAP, established in 2023, is a landmark program that will help ADB accelerate much-needed climate financing. Its initial ambition of $3 billion in guarantees using a leveraged guarantee mechanism could create up to $15 billion in new climate investment.
>
> **Energy Transition Mechanism.** The ETM was launched in 2021 in partnership with the governments of Indonesia and the Philippines and will prepare feasibility studies in Kazakhstan, Pakistan, and Viet Nam. In line with the Paris Agreement, it seeks to reduce greenhouse gas emissions from the power sector by bringing forward the retirement or repurposing of plants powered by fossil fuels, while boosting the share of clean energy in the electricity systems of developing member countries deploying the ETM. It will do so by mobilizing through concessional capital large amounts of commercial funds, thereby creating a pool of blended capital to finance individual transactions.
>
> **ASEAN Catalytic Green Finance Facility.** The ACGF was launched in 2019 by member governments of the Association of Southeast Asian Nations as their regional green finance vehicle. Managed from the start by ADB, the ACGF is a one-stop shop to identify, develop, and finance climate projects by integrating support for upstream planning and downstream project financing. Nine financing partners have so far pledged $1.9 billion in cofinancing, half of it allocated to projects and technical assistance.
>
> **Climate Action Catalyst Fund.** The CACF will work with its development partners to mobilize all-important carbon finance through the purchase of internationally transferred mitigation outcomes under Article 6 of the Paris Agreement. It will catalyze investment in transformative climate action and help developing member countries achieve their nationally determined contribution targets cost-effectively—and to enhance them over time. Initiated in 2022, the CACF is expected to be capitalized with about $100 million in financial commitments and commence operation in 2023.
>
> Source: Asian Development Bank.

ADB will strengthen knowledge partnerships for climate change. It needs to rapidly adopt new ways of designing and financing development projects, incorporating rapidly evolving scientific knowledge and practices to harness evidence-based solutions in response to climate impacts. ADB will continue to build on its convening power in the region to share knowledge, including on the application of latest technologies; facilitate South–South knowledge sharing on best practices; and join forces with other leading institutions in the climate space to play a proactive and supportive role as the research and knowledge partner of choice for DMCs on core aspects of the climate agenda. It will explore sector-specific and cross-sector knowledge partnerships for climate action, such as the Community Resilience Partnership Program (Box 2).

Regional cooperation will build strong coalitions to address the regional climate agenda. Acknowledging the role of regional cooperation and integration in addressing national climate challenges, ADB will build on its strong mandate and track record of supporting regional cooperation to deliver development results and draw on this experience to help DMCs address transboundary climate challenges and solutions, notably through regional strategy dialogue and formulation; data, information, and knowledge sharing; and regional green technology transfer, including through support for international trade and foreign direct investment.

> **Box 2: Community Resilience Partnership Program**
>
> The Community Resilience Partnership Program was established in 2021 to help developing member countries and communities to scale up investments in climate adaptation, especially those that explicitly target the nexus of climate change, poverty, and gender. Implementation is through close partnership with a wide array of stakeholders, including women's groups and civil society, to ensure that resilience solutions enjoy local ownership, are economically and socially just, and inspire further action. As of mid-2023, ADB had mobilized $64 million for the program, which covers all developing member countries with an initial focus on Bangladesh, Cambodia, Indonesia, Nepal, and Tonga.
>
> Source: Asian Development Bank.

ADB will continue close coordination with development partners. As an active partner in joint MDB initiatives, ADB will proactively develop joint knowledge products and guidance on low-carbon and climate-resilient development. It will work with development partners, including multilateral climate funds, and build on their work to develop regional, national, and subnational capacity.

New partnership models combine financing with knowledge partnerships. ADB is considering establishing a series of hubs in areas important for climate mitigation and adaptation. Hubs will link ADB and partners, including civil society, with technical, business, and financial expertise and networks to identify feasible and sustainable solutions that can benefit from finance packages structured as regional and global public goods. Combining technological best practices and innovative finance, these efforts will provide scalable and replicable models for new projects. In addition, the hubs will provide TA and mobilize dedicated concessional finance (Box 3).

Engagement with civil society organizations will be deepened. ADB will work to remove systemic barriers to meaningful partnership with civil society organizations (CSOs) and communities on the climate agenda. It will (i) deepen collaboration with CSOs for local community engagement to ensure that climate work is informed by a range of stakeholder voices, in particular those communities most vulnerable to climate change; (ii) remove internal barriers obstructing collaboration with CSOs under its own processes and requirements; (iii) work with CSOs to help affected workers and communities mitigate impacts and increase opportunities; (iv) expand opportunities for knowledge exchange and capacity building to help CSOs monitor local climate investments, with an emphasis on innovative, community-led methodologies that boost transparency and good governance in climate investments; and (v) engage with women's rights organizations to ensure the participation of women and girls in climate action.

Partnership to address the loss and damage agenda. ADB will play a proactive and supporting role with its partners on the loss and damage agenda, which will help DMCs deal with damage from extreme weather events such as tropical storms and droughts, as well as pernicious slow-onset economic and other losses as climate change raises sea levels, hits agricultural productivity, and compromises freshwater supplies. This is part of a wider finance architecture evolving as agreed at the 27th session of the Conference of the Parties of the UNFCCC (COP27). In addition, ADB will support measures to avert and minimize loss and damage, such as strengthening climate and disaster risk assessment and management for better development planning.

> **Box 3: Leveraging finance and knowledge partnerships**
>
> **Nature Solutions Finance Hub.** ADB intends to seek out and raise investment in nature-based solutions across Asia and the Pacific by developing demonstration projects that show financial structuring that is scalable and bankable. Building on commitments under the COP26 Joint Statement on Nature by multilateral development banks, the hub will demonstrate how ADB and public funds can use payment for ecosystem services, forest or nature bonds, and debt-for-nature swaps to leverage capital investment from foundations, commercial banks, and private investors. The hub will fund nature-based solutions that are impactful, scalable, and crosscutting.
>
> **Hindu Kush Himalya Initiative in Bhutan and Nepal.** This is an example of ADB using enhanced risk management to strengthen risk-informed decision making and leverage insurance to help meet funding needs. The Hindu Kush Himalaya has the world's largest ice reserves outside of the polar regions and is highly exposed to disasters, which climate change is making more frequent and intense. ADB will help Bhutan and Nepal better integrate climate and disaster risk into public and private sector decision making and investment planning. ADB will enhance risk assessment for better design of low-carbon and climate-resilient projects and programs and to link these pipelines to public and private climate finance.
>
> **ADB-Korea Climate Technology Hub.** ADB and the Government of the Republic of Korea have agreed to work towards establishing an ADB–Korea Climate Technology Hub in Seoul to connect developing member countries to cutting-edge climate technology, experts, service providers, and other stakeholders in the climate tech ecosystem. The hub will provide developing member countries access to the latest climate technology, interact with the technology providers, explore cooperation, improve policy environment and ecosystems, and make informed decisions on technology solutions.
>
> Source: Asian Development Bank.

2.2 Upscaling ADB climate investment and its impact

Climate change is experienced globally, but benefits from climate action are seldom fully monetized. Reduced GHG emissions and strengthened climate resilience are public goods. Concessional finance can provide incentives for countries to invest in projects and support policies to strengthen mitigation and adaptation. Most climate investments incur costs in the short term but offer long-term benefits. Mismatch in the timing of costs and benefits makes it a challenge to access finance markets for such investments. In response, ADB has developed a coordinated approach to climate financing, set out below.

ADB will prioritize climate action in its core support for regional and global public goods. The ADB midterm review of Strategy 2030 will develop a refined vision and approach to better support global, regional, and country development priorities, paying particular attention to ADB's role in providing global public goods. ADB will identify key issues and processes involved in differentiating its approach according to countries' climate needs and opportunities. As part of the 14th replenishment of the Asian Development Fund (ADF 14), ADB is working with donors to secure additional dedicated concessional resources for global and regional public goods, including responses to climate change. It will increase impact from ADB climate investments through an improved operational approach and catalyze public and private capital for climate investment by mobilizing the private sector and domestic resources.

Through a more programmatic approach that mainstreams climate change in its operations, ADB will strengthen investment impact. A programmatic and strategic approach will enable ADB to properly sequence and combine a range of interventions to facilitate economy-wide change. This approach will integrate policy, planning, and cross-sector interventions to encourage policy actions for implementing NDCs and long-term strategies, followed by financing support for downstream investment. It will ensure that sovereign operations help DMCs drive private capital mobilization for climate investment and enable the integration of green and blue finance and related frameworks toward achieving development goals.

ADB will continue to diversify its lending framework to incentivize DMC climate investment. ADB approved capital management reform that unlocks $100 billion in new funding capacity over the next decade in response to evolving challenges in the region, including climate change. The expansion of available funds will be leveraged by mobilizing private and domestic capital required to tackle the climate crisis. ADB will explore more concessional terms for climate projects and introduce new financing products that incentivize high-impact, transformative climate projects offering regional and global public goods. Good examples of such financing products and structures are the sustainability-linked loans and bonds currently being deployed by ADB private sector operations, and potential new financing structures, such as payment for ecosystem services and debt-for-climate swaps.

ADB is evaluating how to increase concessional finance and resources for climate finance, notably by expanding the ADF thematic pool and other sources. The implications on resource availability of providing more concessional financing from ADB's own resources will be carefully considered, to ensure that scarce concessional resources are directed to low-income countries and public goods. Concessional resources directed by proper policies will be especially important for incentivizing investment in climate adaptation and disaster resilience (Box 4). Countries with heightened exposure and vulnerability to climate hazards and low capacity to adapt to environmental change need special consideration that acknowledges the disproportionate challenges these countries and their private companies face in accessing climate finance. An approach that considers economic, environmental, and social dimensions will improve resource allocation, as will enhanced capacity development, especially for SIDSs and FCASs.

Box 4: ADF 13 Thematic Pool: Supporting disaster risk reduction and climate adaptation

The thematic pool under the 13th replenishment of the Asian Development Fund (ADF 13) is tailored to address the most critical challenges facing the poorest and most vulnerable developing member countries. Aligned with Strategy 2030, the thematic pool focuses on three strategic areas: (i) fostering regional cooperation and integration, including the provision of regional public goods; (ii) supporting disaster risk reduction and climate adaptation; and (iii) achieving Sustainable Development Goal 5, on a transformative gender agenda. Under the second strategic area, support extends beyond standard climate mainstreaming toward designing innovative standalone projects whose primary objective is to build shock and natural hazard resilience. During 2021–2023, ADF 13 Thematic Pool commitments under this strategic area amounted to $63.1 million. This was 37% of all thematic pool commitments to date, amply on track to meet the 25% target for the entirety of the ADF 13 period, from 2021 to 2024.

Source: Asian Development Bank.

ADB will improve the quality of its operations and climate financing. Critical elements that need to be introduced into climate financing systems include incentive systems to spur higher contributions to achieve climate outcomes on key performance indicators, such as GHG emission reduction and the number of people made more resilient, that outstrip investment value. ADB will consider establishing a categorization system designed to encourage projects and programs with highly beneficial impact and potential to contribute to transformational climate outcomes.[20]

---

[20] Any categorization system for climate will incorporate lessons from ADB's gender categorization system. If a system is successfully introduced, programs and projects in the top climate categories may receive preferential access to funds, streamlined business processes, and concessional resources.

Technical assistance will facilitate transformational change. TA is key to building a pipeline of transformative projects and programs in the region. It can support systematic policy dialogue with DMCs and enhance the monitoring of project implementation, which are critical to correctly directing and rolling out coherent climate action. ADB will use more TA clusters and facilities to pool resources toward developing a pipeline of integrated climate investments. It is important to focus on TA and upstream work with governments on policies, legal frameworks, and incentives to support and create an enabling environment for projects originating in the private sector. Recognizing the importance of climate action in upper-middle-income countries, ADB will explore how to mobilize TA grants for climate action beyond countries in groups A and B to those in group C, which are ordinarily ineligible for concessionary assistance. TA will also be used to incentivize private clients to go beyond business as usual with their climate ambition, and to amplify development impact and climate outcomes.[21]

Carbon finance can incentivize investment in low-carbon technology and reduce GHG emissions. International carbon markets under Article 6 of the Paris Agreement and the voluntary carbon market can attract from both the public and the private sector much-needed innovative carbon finance to incentivize and catalyze investment in low-carbon technology. ADB will continue its integrated approach through its Carbon Market Program by providing upstream technical capacity building to public and private stakeholders and mobilizing downstream carbon finance (Box 5). It will maximize carbon finance opportunities to provide additional sources of finance to enhance viability and incentivize investment in low-carbon technologies, including those mitigating GHGs with high global warming potential, such as methane and hydrofluorocarbons.

Box 5: ADB's Carbon Market Program

ADB has long engaged with carbon markets, allowing it to build strong expertise in carbon pricing. Trust funds have been important vehicles through which ADB mobilizes carbon finance, notably the Asia Pacific Carbon Fund, Future Carbon Fund, and Japan Fund for the Joint Crediting Mechanism. The Carbon Market Program supports carbon pricing initiatives and carbon market development in developing member countries through the Technical Support Facility and the Article 6 Support Facility, which provide support for technical, capacity, and policy development. The Carbon Market Program has evolved in response to the Paris Agreement and the changing architecture of international carbon markets. Under Carbon Market 2.0, ADB continues to mobilize carbon finance and incentivize investment in low-carbon technology through domestic, bilateral, and international carbon markets and to provide technical, capacity-building, and knowledge support to developing member countries.

Source: Asian Development Bank.

ADB's new operating model reorients its support for climate action toward private sector development. ADB will ensure greater synergy between sovereign and nonsovereign operations. Sovereign operations, including policy-based lending, can drive private capital mobilization and enable effective development outcomes. ADB's impact is maximized when it provides properly sequenced and coordinated solutions that support policy and regulatory reform, develop an enabling environment, and provide transaction advisory and project-preparation support, direct investment, and cofinancing. Similarly, ADB private sector operations can identify opportunities to respond more proactively to commercial and other barriers to climate action. Insights and feedback from the private sector should feed into the design of better public policies and better sovereign projects, aiming to mobilize more private sector capital for climate action.

---

[21] For example, TA support is essential to help smallholder farmers shrink their carbon footprint, invest in natural capital, and become more climate resilient.

Nonsovereign financing for climate will be expanded. ADB will continue to align its private sector portfolio and PPP activities with its climate ambitions. It will expand on its provision of climate finance investment in a client-responsive way. This may include greater use of innovative and scalable approaches to impact-focused lending, such as transition financing and sustainability-linked loans, as well as supporting international trade, global supply chains, and capital market investment.

ADB will adopt a holistic approach to mobilizing private capital. It is developing a private sector strategy for integration into all processes used to prepare country partnership strategies and indicative country pipeline and monitoring reports. To further catalyze a pipeline of low-carbon and climate-resilient private sector projects, ADB will continue to help DMCs develop transparent and effective legal and regulatory frameworks, and thus generate enabling environments for private sector finance. In addition, by proactively preparing low-carbon and climate-resilient projects, ADB can create a pipeline of PPP projects able to access green and blue finance. Further, ADB will maximize opportunities to mobilize carbon finance and render more attractive private sector investment opportunities in low-carbon technologies and solutions, and through guarantee and risk-sharing instruments to mobilize private sector capital.

In line with MDB blended finance principles, ADB will coordinate with partners to scale up the use of blended finance. Blended finance can continue to play an important role in accelerating and scaling up climate ambition in Asia and the Pacific. As blended resources need to be allocated according to the climate benefits that the operation will generate, greater focus will be placed on projects that can be replicated at scale. This will require engagement with bilateral and multilateral donors, philanthropies, and national financing agencies.

2.3 ADB's internal knowledge management and research

Knowledge management, capacity development, and research are pivotal to advancing an inherently complex and urgent ADB climate agenda. Effectively addressing climate challenges demands interdisciplinary collaboration, evidence-based solutions, and learning. Resources must therefore be allocated under the action plan to develop skills in deep knowledge management and its application through tailored tools.

ADB will enhance its management of data, information, and knowledge. It is committed to ensure that climate action is evidence-based and robust, grounded on access for ADB and its DMCs to the latest climate data, modeling tools, and spatial information and their strengthened utilization in decision-making processes. To achieve this, ADB is building an ADB data management platform, deploying its Digital Record Management System, and aligning its knowledge management with International Organization for Standardization Standard 40301. The central goal is to ensure seamless access to climate data, information, and knowledge for employees precisely when they need it. A dedicated focus on refining climate change taxonomy will establish a well-governed information architecture conducive to interdisciplinary collaboration, efficient knowledge identification, secure storage, and effortless knowledge discovery and reuse. This robust information architecture will underline a forthcoming ADB knowledge navigator, paving the way for digital knowledge management enabled by artificial intelligence.

ADB will generate knowledge solutions for climate change. ADB's strategic emphasis is to deliver knowledge solutions tailored to address the pressing issue of climate change. It has optimized its business processes to align knowledge support from within the institution with actual DMC demand, facilitated by country knowledge plans that devise knowledge-driven solutions for specific development challenges, with a particular focus on addressing climate change. These solutions span upstream planning, midstream implementation, and downstream impact, emphasizing the integration of solutions across diverse sectors and themes. ADB will prioritize the documentation of lessons learned, case studies, and impact evaluations to ensure that an accessible climate agenda and new climate projects and programs facilitate knowledge transfer and continuous improvement.

ADB will further develop capacity in DMC counterparts and its own staff. Capacity to address climate change necessarily entails development planning, investment decision making, and project design and implementation. ADB will advance climate leadership training and provide sector- and theme-specific climate training programs for staff, with the design goal of co-learning with and among DMCs. This requires ADB to gain better oversight of capacity development, improve collaboration with external partners, and thus enhance the delivery and monitoring of these efforts. Through country engagement, ADB will move away from ad hoc climate capacity development toward programmatic approaches.

ADB is committed to nurturing and championing innovation to advance its climate agenda. An ADB-wide innovation hub was recently inaugurated to provide staff with opportunities to explore novel avenues for collaboration and apply methodologies such as design thinking, strategic foresight, and innovation challenges. This initiative will play a crucial role in identifying worthy climate pilot projects and forging partnerships to amplify climate achievements. Moreover, the hub will facilitate the incorporation of pertinent technological developments in climate change, social innovations in behavioral science, insights from industry, and climate policy research recommendations.

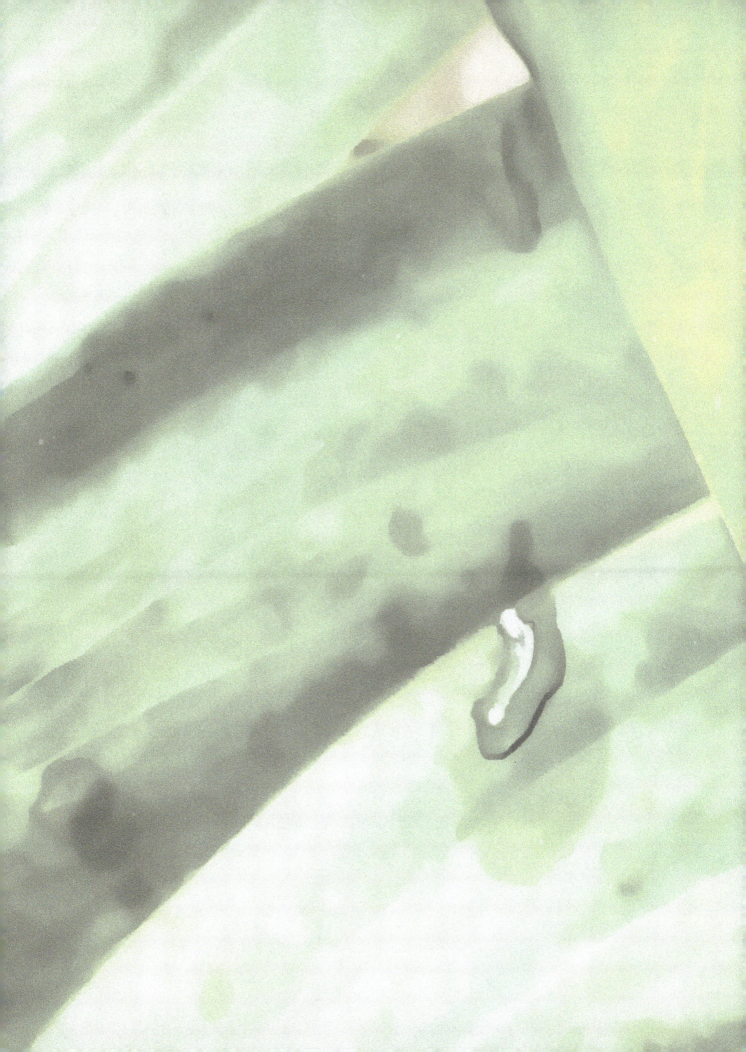

3 How we engage: ADB country engagement for climate action

ADB engagement with DMC national governments is central to its climate work. ADB will help DMCs deliver climate-responsive economic and social development through high-quality sovereign and nonsovereign operations. It will enhance DMC readiness for climate action by supporting policy and institutional reform and by producing knowledge to support partners' understanding of climate risks and opportunities for transition.

A fully integrated package on climate change combines sovereign and nonsovereign solutions. Increasingly, ADB will integrate sovereign and nonsovereign work at the country level, often using sovereign entry points to create space for private sector innovation and solutions provided at scale. Similarly, ADB can use lessons from private sector projects to inform sovereign interventions. ADB will complement country-specific work with support for DMC collective efforts to address transboundary and regional climate challenges.

ADB will approach each DMC differently. It will adopt tailored approaches, particularly for FCASs, SIDSs, and mountainous countries. In these countries, vulnerability and fragility stem from heightened exposure to risk and insufficient coping capacity to manage, absorb, or mitigate it. Risk can be exacerbated by geographical constraints, small human resource pools, weak institutions, and worsening impacts from compounded risks and hazards. These factors hamper the efficiency, effectiveness, and sustainability of development efforts, requiring a differentiated approach to assistance. Such an approach is consistent with ADB's Strategy 2030; its Pacific Approach, 2021–2025;[22] its FCAS and SIDS approach (Box 6); and activities such as the Hindu Kush Himalaya Initiative in Bhutan and Nepal (Box 3).[23]

ADB will offer upstream, midstream, and downstream support for comprehensive climate change solutions at the country level. Upstream, it will offer knowledge and policy solutions; midstream, support to ensure that solutions are embedded within core institutions, national plans and budgets, and procurement processes; and downstream, sovereign and nonsovereign operations.

---

[22] ADB. 2021. *Pacific Approach, 2021–2025*.
[23] ADB. 2021. *Fragile and Conflict-Affected Situations and Small Island Developing States Approach*.

> **Box 6: Differentiated approach for the Pacific**
>
> ADB support for its 12 small Pacific island developing member countries reflects its commitment to a differentiated approach that supports a resilient Pacific. Three priority areas feature prominently in the Pacific approach at the nexus of climate change, disaster risk management, and sustainability:
>
> (i) **Support inclusive and resilient growth.** Strengthen business environments and invest in growth sectors, while supporting the sustainable management of ecosystems. Leverage revenue to expand economic foundations, in particular by supporting shared goals for healthy and productive oceans and enhancing the resilience of poor and vulnerable groups.
> (ii) **Deliver sustainable services.** Fund the construction and expansion of basic infrastructure that underpins inclusive development and ensures greater resilience under climate change and in the wake of disasters. Support long-term spatial planning that considers climate scenarios over the medium and long term and appropriately expand water and sanitation services to benefit local communities.
> (iii) **Prepare for and respond to shocks.** Collect, analyze, and use risk data to inform policy and long-term planning. Deliver quick-disbursing assistance in the wake of disasters, provide contingent disaster finance, facilitate access to climate finance, and support the implementation of nationally determined contributions and national adaptation plans.
>
> In the 12 small Pacific island states and in Fiji and Papua New Guinea, ADB will advance its ongoing work in these three priority areas through a differentiated, collaborative approach in line with established regional architecture for the Pacific and its development community. Leveraging ADB's existing regional and local presence, the approach will facilitate greater access to global climate funds using flexible procurement models and streamlined client reporting. ADB will review safeguard approaches and explore how best to provide support on the ground for upstream diagnostics and project preparation and implementation.
>
> Source: Asian Development Bank.

3.1 Upstream: Strategic engagement for enhanced policy frameworks

ADB will deepen upstream engagement in research, analysis, and advice to enhance national and regional policy frameworks for climate change. DMCs need strong national policy frameworks to promote low-carbon development, enhance climate and disaster resilience, and strengthen disaster risk management. Where there are competing policies and investment priorities, institutional processes should prioritize climate action. This requires a mindset shift that sees the transition to a low-carbon economy as an opportunity for economic growth, not a trade-off with it. ADB must champion this shift by showcasing solutions that achieve climate and sustainable development goals alike, and that demonstrate the importance of early investment in adaptation and climate resilience to reduce future economic losses from climate change.

Climate change will be further integrated into ADB country partnership and regional strategies. ADB will carry this climate focus beyond the framing of its strategy into all aspects of its work by enhancing the capacity of country and project teams to identify opportunities for climate action and by following these opportunities through to design, financing, and implementation. Country partnership strategies will outline how ADB will support the climate agenda in a country through integrated upstream, midstream, and downstream support. This will be sustained through training and recruitment to ensure that ADB staff on the ground can lead dialogue with DMCs on climate change throughout the programing cycle. To support this dialogue, ADB will further develop its climate action toolkit with eligible climate activities.

ADB support will strengthen DMC climate ambitions. NDCs, long-term strategies, and national adaptation plans will be aligned with and integrated into development policies and planning systems that are systematically supported to enhance climate ambition over time, in line with the Paris Agreement. ADB will use policy-based loans to strengthen DMC policy frameworks on climate change, complementing this at the midstream stage by embedding climate policy in national budgets and planning processes. It will support these processes with TA, capacity building, technological innovations, and financing that helps countries identify mitigation and adaptation measures, establish baselines and targets, and develop implementation plans. ADB will work with sector policy makers to strengthen sector capacity for climate action and embed NDC and national adaptation plan targets in sector investments (Box 7).

Box 7: Enhancing climate change ambitions through nationally determined contributions

NDC Advance is a technical assistance platform established by ADB to help developing member countries (DMCs) mobilize finance, build capacity, and acquire knowledge and other support to implement their nationally determined contributions (NDCs). The objectives of the platform are to (i) help DMCs refine and enhance climate ambitions, translate NDCs into climate investment plans, and identify priority climate projects that may be executed with ADB assistance; (ii) improve DMC access to external public and private climate finance, including funding for innovative financing mechanisms to support NDC implementation; (iii) develop tools to measure, monitor, and report on commitments made under NDCs; and (iv) help DMCs identify the climate adaptation investments and policy and institutional reforms needed to unlock barriers to implementing investments in climate adaptation.

Source: Asian Development Bank.

ADB will step up assistance to DMCs that creates dynamic business environments able to attract private sector climate investment. ADB will help DMCs attract high-quality private sector investment for climate initiatives in a sustainable manner. It will be innovative and creative in this endeavor, combining sovereign and nonsovereign approaches with specific sector and thematic expertise. Further, it will help DMCs design fiscal policies that provide incentives for the private sector to invest in low-carbon and climate-resilient infrastructure.

Using its regional mandate, ADB will drive climate action. Regional cooperation is crucial for framing regional challenges in regional dialogue toward agreement on collective action, including policy coordination, agenda setting, and regional analyses for cross-border concerns. ADB will draw on its mandate for and experience in regional cooperation to help DMCs find solutions to regional climate challenges by providing TA for regional solutions, building regional platforms for enhanced project design and financing, and supporting regional action on climate change. It will explore support to make major global supply chains anchored in Asia and the Pacific low carbon and climate resilient. Taking into consideration regional trade and investment agreements, ADB will advance DMC understanding of how climate-related border pricing adjustment made by other countries affects their economy. Carbon tracking and reporting across global supply chains could enable a competitive advantage for the Asia and the Pacific, as well as attract climate finance (Boxes 8 and 9).

> **Box 8: Regional climate action through Central Asia Regional Economic Cooperation**
>
> ADB supported a scoping study to assess how Central Asia Regional Economic Cooperation members can address climate issues through regional cooperation. The study will inform the preparation of a climate vision to be adopted by members and an overarching framework to advance subregional action on climate change. Additional resources are being mobilized to support the harmonization of national climate strategies in key areas where regional cooperation is critically important: energy, water, agriculture, transport, and disaster risk management. A steering committee on climate change will be established to discuss regional approaches and develop a road map for climate projects.
>
> Source: Asian Development Bank.

> **Box 9: Regional multi-hazard climate and disaster risk assessments**
>
> To expand pipelines for effective investment in climate adaptation, ADB supports multi-hazard climate and disaster risk assessments in the Pacific. These assessments produce locally specific, geo-referenced data on projected climate change and disaster impacts from, for example, sea level rise and changing temperatures. Assessments are developed and implemented in close coordination with national governments to address priority concerns and build on existing data and knowledge. Assessments range from a focus on the urban centers of Nuku'alofa in Tonga (completed in 2021) and Luganville in Vanuatu (under way) to concentrating on key public assets and systems such as the international port and airport in Ararua, Cook Islands (under way). For the port and airport, indirect losses associated with interrupted flows of goods and services are also investigated for a better understanding of the centrality of these assets to small island developing states. The information gained through assessments is fed into the design and implementation of adaptation plans and projects, and into post-disaster damage and needs assessments and recovery plans.
>
> Source: Asian Development Bank.

ADB will work with DMCs to ensure that the transition to low-carbon and climate-resilient economies is just. It will help DMCs embed a just transition in their policy frameworks and, to this end, engage with civil society, communities, and youth at the country level. The effort will promote intergenerational equity and social inclusion to ensure that the transition considers the needs of marginalized and vulnerable communities. ADB will work with DMCs to support low-carbon manufacturing that generates green jobs, and to ensure that workers have the necessary skills and that firms have access to finance to participate in the low-carbon transition. ADB will support DMC efforts to develop adaptive and responsive social protection to protect women, poor and vulnerable populations, people with disabilities, the elderly, and young people during the transition.

Recognizing that climate change affects women and men differently, ADB will put gender at the center of its climate agenda. ADB will work with DMCs to integrate gender equality and women's empowerment into national policies and programs. Women need to participate in decision-making processes to ensure that climate policies recognize that women often bear a greater burden from climate change in their traditional roles as caregivers, farmers, and food providers. ADB will strengthen women's climate resilience, having learned from regional experience with COVID-19 and other crises that such shocks often affect women and young people disproportionately through lost livelihoods, heavier burdens of family care and other unpaid work, and worsened exposure to gender-based violence.

ADB will hardwire climate change into country programming. This will begin with more in-depth geographic and sector climate change diagnostics, building on diagnostics already available that identify binding constraints and the most critical actions needed to enable ADB operations in each country to progress on climate change (Box 10). Targeted upstream analysis on critical climate issues will seek out practical avenues for progress, leveraging ADB's convening power and forward thinking to develop long-term solutions for DMCs. ADB will approach programming in a way that puts coordination at its core by approaching partnerships through a country climate development platform in which development partners including ADB share out responsibilities according to their expertise.

Box 10: Operationalizing Paris Agreement alignment in country programming processes

To effectively help ADB developing member countries (DMCs) achieve the objectives of the Paris Agreement, it is imperative to enhance their ability to identify and execute appropriate investments. Investments must align with both the Paris Agreement and DMCs' own long-term strategies to reduce greenhouse gas emissions and foster climate-resilient development. With a dedicated technical assistance program, ADB will facilitate country dialogue, conduct analyses, and devise strategies to ensure that alignment with the Paris Agreement becomes standard in future country partnership strategies and country programming. This will build on existing efforts and coordination with other multilateral development banks. It will also verify project congruity with DMCs' Paris-aligned development pathways in discussions and deliberations initiated early in the project cycle. This strategy fundamentally requires enhanced ability to generate an upstream pipeline of operations in line with the Paris Agreement. It entails bolstering capacity in DMCs to unify government departments around climate objectives, recognize financing opportunities, and develop project requests that adhere to such goals and pathways.

Source: Asian Development Bank.

3.2 Midstream: Embedding climate action in core institutions and national systems

ADB will help DMCs integrate climate action into public finance management, especially budget processes and public procurement systems. Climate action needs to be a priority during strategic planning and the development of national fiscal frameworks. Prioritization should be reflected across DMC institutions, starting with ministries of finance, and including subnational governments, regulatory bodies, and state-owned enterprises. ADB will support the adoption of frameworks that facilitate assessments of public finance management in light of climate change, looking at public expenditure, financial accountability, and risks to public procurement processes posed by climate change.

DMCs need clear financing strategies to support climate action. Financing strategies should be part of the national budget process and be reflected in medium-term fiscal frameworks, investment plans, and national development frameworks. ADB will strengthen DMC access to climate finance, including from their own fiscal resources built up through efficient domestic resource mobilization and by phasing out fossil fuel subsidies (Box 11). With a redoubled focus on carbon pricing as carbon markets mature and become increasingly important sources of finance, ADB will help DMCs develop appropriate taxes, trading systems for domestic emissions, and incentive structures that allow them to benefit from these markets. Further, ADB will mobilize concessional climate finance from donors and international climate funds, as well as continue to work with DMCs to leverage private sector finance through enhanced support for PPP and scaled-up and streamlined access to blended finance.

> **Box 11: Enhancing climate action through domestic resource mobilization**
>
> The Asia Pacific Tax Hub is a platform that provides technical assistance and capacity building to support tax policy and administration. The hub aims to enhance domestic resource mobilization, which is crucial to increasing finance for climate action. It helps developing member countries develop and implement tax policies and administrative systems that raise revenue for climate action, in particular environmental taxes and fiscal incentives for investment in renewable energy and energy efficiency. Further, it builds national capacity in international good practice governing climate taxation. ADB will use this to help developing member countries phase out fossil fuel subsidies and set and implement carbon pricing at the full social cost of carbon.
>
> Source: Asian Development Bank.

To safeguard fiscal balances, ADB will leverage insurance for investments in resilience. National development plans must consider greater climate and disaster risks by preparing comprehensive multi-hazard assessments and analyses to achieve inclusive policy responses and cost-effectively manage risk. Insurance obtained through blue and green bonds for climate investment can significantly contribute to meeting post-disaster funding needs, protect fiscal balances, and further development objectives. In addition, innovative insurance solutions can strengthen resilience by (i) reducing credit risk and thus rendering affordable necessary investments in climate and disaster protection, mitigation, and adaptation projects; (ii) giving debtors more financial leeway to carry out emergency relief and reconstruction in the event of a disaster; and (iii) making government or corporate finances more shock resilient. Further, insurance can mobilize private capital investment by making climate investment less risky.

Countries' ability to integrate climate plans with sector policies and plans, road maps, and projects will be strengthened. Integrating sector plans with NDCs, national adaptation plans, and national fiscal frameworks will require the development of climate project pipelines, the embedding of climate solutions in sector approaches, and the exploration of multisector solutions. ADB will help DMCs translate NDCs and national adaptation plans into practical operations by developing climate mitigation and adaptation projects. It will work with other international finance institutions to strengthen green infrastructure governance in line with G20 initiatives.[24] Diagnostics are expected to consider climate change impacts, and sector road maps should include climate-related solutions. Maximizing development impact is a major focus.

ADB will invest in research to reflect climate change in economic analysis used to support decision-making. It will strengthen methods of valuing natural capital and climate benefits by seeking alternative approaches to discounting future costs and benefits, and by improving analysis of the social costs of carbon. ADB will explore ways to use economic tools more flexibly, beyond traditional cost–benefit analysis, to inform climate decisions.

ADB will step up sovereign pipeline development in DMCs to make them more low carbon and climate resilient. It will mobilize additional TA funds to support the design of such investments and more concessional finance to bear some of the financial costs to DMCs of project design. Knowing that fiscal policy plays a critical role in responding to climate change, ADB will develop DMC capacity to develop climate-focused fiscal policies. Effective upstream and midstream work on the knowledge and sovereign side facilitate the longer-term pipeline of private sector projects.

Bankable projects in greater numbers can attract private sector climate investment. ADB will work with public and private sector actors in DMCs to address barriers to the development of more low-carbon and climate-resilient nonsovereign projects. This can be achieved by discovering how a deficient enabling environment may limit potential for climate investment. To this end, it will continue to develop blended finance able to de-risk projects that are already

---

[24] The Coalition of Finance Ministers for Climate Action, bringing together fiscal and economic policy makers from over 70 countries, recently proposed ways to spearhead the global transition toward low-carbon and climate-resilient economic development.

close to being bankable and to redouble upstream efforts to improve the business environment. ADB will complement this through continued efforts to enhance PPP frameworks in DMCs and transaction advisory support for individual PPPs that offer opportunities for climate finance. It will help DMCs strengthen their finance frameworks for climate investment through green and climate financing initiatives and by increasing trade-related financing capacity, explicitly targeting sustainable and climate-aligned trade financing and guarantees.

ADB will help DMCs embed climate change in national budgets and planning and procurement processes. Applicable modalities at the midstream stage include policy-based lending (Box 12), sector development programs, contingent disaster financing (Box 13), results-based lending, and policy-based guarantees. Programmatic approaches can sustain momentum on climate action, and enhanced institutional mechanisms can improve cross-government coordination and multi-stakeholder platforms. ADB will complement these efforts with targeted TA to empower public officials in DMCs to apply good practice when implementing climate-focused regulation and mainstreaming climate policy. Further, ADB will enhance monitoring and evaluation frameworks with improved systems for data collection, analysis, and monitoring.

Box 12: Policy-based lending that drives climate action

The Philippines Climate Change Action Program is ADB's first dedicated policy-based climate loan. Approved and completed in 2022, the first subprogram provided $250 million to the Government of the Philippines for the implementation of national climate policies—including the fulfilment of the nationally determined contribution, which targets peak greenhouse gas emissions by 2030—and the scaling up of climate adaptation and mitigation and disaster resilience. The program strengthens efforts to transform toward low-carbon and climate-resilient sectors that are national priorities for climate action, targeting adaptation in highly vulnerable sectors like agriculture, natural resources, and the environment, and mitigation in such emission-intensive sectors as energy and transport. Reform under the program aims to reinforce planning, financing, and institutional linkages for climate action; enhance climate resilience; and strengthen low-carbon pathways.

Source: Asian Development Bank.

Box 13: Contingent disaster financing in the Pacific

With the Pacific Disaster Resilience Program, ADB promotes climate resilience in two ways. First, the program offers fast-disbursing and flexible funding to help countries deal with the residual risks of weather extremes magnified by climate change. These funds can be used to speed up recovery in highly vulnerable communities. They also help countries avoid having to reallocate funds from social programs to cope with disasters, which would deliver a double blow to the vulnerable. Second, following the policy-based lending modality, the program promotes reform that enhances climate resilience through risk-sensitive development strategies; sector-specific plans, tools, and codes; and financial preparedness to deal with impacts from climate-induced disasters. Piloted in 2016 and now in its fourth phase, the program has gained traction in the Pacific and become an important instrument with which island states manage their financial exposure to climate risks.

Source: Asian Development Bank.

3.3 Downstream: High-quality operations and implementation

ADB will scale up the number, size, and quality of climate projects and programs in its operations in line with MDB principles and methodologies. It will continue direct support for sovereign and nonsovereign clients through investment into sectors that will be key to decarbonization and adaptation, notably energy, transport, infrastructure and the built environment, agriculture, manufacturing, mining, and other industries. ADB nonsovereign operations will assess opportunities for more ambitious origination and mobilization of climate finance across its DMCs. It will undertake enhanced climate risk screening of projects, mainstream standards of project alignment with the Paris Agreement, and develop capacity in clients to do likewise. ADB will provide TA to sovereign and nonsovereign clients to improve their understanding of decarbonization opportunities and help them manage their exposure to transition and physical risks.

Central to strong operations are enhanced project preparation, implementation, and maintenance. ADB is committed to improving the quality of project preparation, including through PPP, to enhance the supply of investable projects for low-carbon and climate-resilient infrastructure. On the sovereign side, ADB will support DMC efforts to put climate considerations at the heart of project and program preparation and will mobilize additional TA resources to support the integration of climate components and improve standards for project design, such as resource efficiency and green infrastructure standards. To maximize impact, ADB will explore extending this support to group C countries, which are ordinarily ineligible for concessionary assistance.

ADB will continue to improve its guidelines for high-quality climate projects. This will ensure that projects and programs appropriately employ proactive stakeholder mapping and engagement, use participatory processes, and include capacity building for local communities, civil society, businesses, and other stakeholders, to continuously engage them in the project or program and thus ensure its long-term sustainability. ADB will enable and help communities and civil society to lead project and program monitoring.

Work with the finance sector will enhance its role in developing climate projects. Green climate finance frameworks will be complemented by green taxonomies and enhanced capacity and awareness. ADB will work with finance institutions to develop green climate finance products and thus ensure financial flows to support innovation and implementation in the climate space. It will work with banks and regulatory authorities to introduce regulations to better manage climate risks to banks and to direct capital toward actors that contribute to low-carbon, climate-resilient futures. ADB will demonstrate leadership in improving disclosure and reporting standards, notably through sustainability reports. In addition, it will help DMCs implement finance and private sector standards on climate change, drawing on its own experience and that of others when aligning with the goals of the Paris Agreement. ADB will continue to be active in trade and trade finance, directly engaging with international and local banks to advance sustainable trade finance and—through involvement with the International Financial Reporting Standards Advisory Council and the affiliated Sustainability Accounting Standards Board—providing strategic leadership through industry associations and shaping the development of standards and regulations pertaining to climate change and sustainability, as well as to environmental, social, and governance concerns.

Sustainable procurement will be promoted. ADB will demonstrate sustainable public procurement and promote the incorporation of sustainability throughout procurement processes and supply chains in projects that it finances. This will be achieved by identifying high-impact areas, setting sustainability requirements and criteria, adopting green specifications and standards and whole-of-life costing, and promoting the adoption of digital solutions for smarter use of resources and low-impact infrastructure. Guidance on incorporating environmental, social, economic, and institutionally sustainable criteria in procurement will be provided during strategic procurement planning and bidding for ADB-financed projects. Considerations of environmental, social, and institutional governance will be incorporated in procurement due diligence and diagnostic assessments at the project and country level. ADB will promote and support the incorporation of sustainable procurement practices in national public procurement frameworks through TA, policy-based lending, and knowledge partnerships. To enhance adoption over the whole infrastructure supply chain, ADB will collaborate with other international organizations, the private sector, training institutions, CSOs, and industry on business outreach and capacity building related to sustainable procurement.

ADB will enhance safeguards to better manage climate risks. ADB environmental and social safeguard requirements recognize that climate change may pose risks to projects, and that projects may exacerbate climate change. Climate change is an important consideration when managing risks and impacts to vulnerable and indigenous peoples and to worker and community health and safety. It is a factor to bear in mind when minimizing (and paying compensation for) any land acquisition and land-use restrictions, and when protecting and conserving biodiversity and ecological functions. Environmental and social assessments should include climate-related risks. GHG monitoring will be a new requirement under ADB's new safeguard policy; where a project emits GHG, ADB will require that alternatives be considered to reduce project emissions. For any project that risks climate impact or worsened climate exposure or vulnerability, ADB will require the climate risk assessment to identify appropriate remedial measures.

The sustainability of climate-resilient infrastructure will be prioritized through efficient operation and adequate maintenance. Project design and procurement methods will consider options to ensure the long-term sustainability of the climate-resilient assets thus created. This will entail adequate training and capacity building to ensure consistent delivery of high-quality service.

4 How we deliver: Advancing low-carbon and climate-resilient solutions across operations

Climate change is a multidimensional challenge that will require multidimensional solutions. It is a crosscutting issue that affects multiple sectors and requires an integrated approach. This section lays out five intervention areas across the full range of ADB sector and thematic work. Sector-specific climate actions are in Appendix 2.

4.1 Integrated climate-smart planning and technology

ADB will pursue holistic approaches to combat climate change and enhance climate and disaster resilience. ADB is well positioned to follow whole-of-economy and whole-of-society approaches, considering its technical expertise in various fields relevant to climate change and its experience in engaging governments, the private sector, CSOs, and other stakeholders. These strengths will be applied to shape comprehensive strategies that address climate change at the local, national, and regional level. ADB can leverage its multisector expertise to support the design and implementation of comprehensive strategies and planning approaches that encompass effective low-carbon and climate risk-reduction planning, forecasting and early warning systems, financial preparedness, communication, stakeholder consultation, and raising awareness and developing capacity in stakeholders.

ADB will strengthen integrated approaches for synergy. Integrated approaches use climate-smart planning practices that mitigate climate change while helping societies to adapt to it. Such synergies are prominent in water, energy, transport, and urban development, as well as across agriculture, food, nature, and rural development. They can have co-benefits such as avoiding biodiversity loss. Synergy requires a shift toward collaborative planning supported by appropriate governance models. Increased engagement with civil society and the private sector when planning projects with various levels of government strengthens social accountability and thereby encourages good governance and social inclusion. It is critical that planning processes highlight climate and sector objectives, forming functional linkages between urban and rural areas and strengthening the sustainability of rural communities and food supply in response to climate change (Box 14).

Box 14: Pakistan: Country Climate Investment Tracker and Visual Guide Dashboard

Pakistan's Country Climate Investment Tracker and Visual Guide Dashboard was initiated in 2022. It was developed with ADB support to monitor climate change trends and visualize direct and indirect impacts across Pakistan. The system is capable of documenting climate knowledge through a tool that populates adaptation and mitigation plans and related achievements toward Pakistan's nationally determined contribution. Further, it interactively elaborates possible adaptation and mitigation solutions and recommends practical means to understand future climate finance needs and make better-informed decisions. In sum, the dashboard is a toolkit for the centralized tracking of adaptation and mitigation investments and their financing.

Source: Asian Development Bank.

Technological progress will be promoted early in planning and design. ADB can catalyze technological progress through strategies and activities that invest in and transfer affordable and emerging technologies, and that employ adequate piloting, testing, and demonstration. ADB can offer TA to countries and projects to adopt and adapt technologies, providing expertise, advisory services, and technical guidance to help identify appropriate technologies, develop implementation plans, and overcome challenges to technological adaptation. As introducing climate-smart technology likely involves training people, skill development must be integral to integrated solutions.

Low-lying and coastal cities are increasingly vulnerable to climate change and need a holistic, climate-smart approach to steer urban planning. ADB will help cities undertake integrated urban planning and pursue low-carbon and climate-resilient development through risk-sensitive land-use management, nature-based climate solutions, integrated water and sanitation management, improved resource efficiency, and low-carbon public transport. Major opportunities for climate-smart planning and development are in the water, energy, and transport sectors. Urban and rural areas alike can benefit from water and energy conservation and efficient use, as well as from carbon capture and sustainable land-use practices (Box 15).

Box 15: Integrated and holistic solutions to urban–rural development challenges

The Aimags and Soums Green Regional Development Investment Program will promote in Mongolia a transformative model for green territorial development and green urban–rural linkages. The $735 million program combines ADB investment with counterpart financing from the Government of Mongolia and the private sector, with cofinancing from the European Investment Bank, European Union, and Green Climate Fund. It will implement climate-resilient carbon sequestration and sustainable rangeland management to empower herder groups to practice sustainable livestock and agricultural management. It will promote renewable energy and low-carbon solutions through urban services, to build livable *aimag* and *soum* municipalities as anchors for a green agribusiness value chain. The program will establish a green and inclusive regional agribusiness fund to finance climate-smart financial mechanisms and institutions and thus break through the financial bottlenecks that constrain small and medium-sized agribusinesses.

Source: Asian Development Bank.

4.2 Inclusive and climate-smart socioeconomic development

Climate change places major strains on inclusive socioeconomic development. DMCs are challenged by inequitable income, asset distribution, and access to services—inequity that climate change deepens through disaster risk. Persistent social and economic inequity is a problem in itself but also hinders the achievement of climate resilience. Climate action therefore requires support for DMC efforts to deliver inclusive climate-smart objectives and a just transition through livelihood strengthening, addressing the needs of women and the poorest and most vulnerable people, and investing in climate-smart education, health, and social protection.

ADB will invest in climate-responsive social protection. Scaling up support for climate resilience should focus in particular on the needs of women, poor and vulnerable populations, people with disabilities, the elderly, and young people. Climate change affects these groups disproportionally, both as a direct consequence of climate impacts and through the distributional effects of climate policies, programs, and investments. ADB will strengthen its support for social protection programs to be informed by robust assessments of climate and disaster risks and the development of inclusive social protection systems that prioritize adaptive shock response. Social protection is similarly key to the social dimension of a just transition, with labor market programs one way to support transitions into new economic activities and address disparity in access (Box 16). ADB will support gender-responsive, pro-poor, and inclusive development and work with CSOs on inclusive and participatory approaches through the project lifecycle. To ensure a just transition, special attention will be paid to the needs of individuals and communities most at risk. Building resilience requires simultaneous and coordinated interventions that take a crosscutting and integrated approach, which requires in turn early investment in knowledge and analytical work, as well as strong collaboration and knowledge sharing across sectors and themes.

Box 16: Bangladesh: Strengthening Social Resilience Program

This policy-based loan supports institutional and policy reform to make social protection in Bangladesh more inclusive and responsive, to protect vulnerable populations from socioeconomic challenges. This is made particularly critical by widespread vulnerability in Bangladesh to climate impacts. Under the program, ADB helps the government strengthen reform to improve the coverage and efficiency of social protection, deepen financial inclusion for disadvantaged people, and strengthen responses to diverse protection needs. Efficiency will be enhanced through system digitalization and integration and the harmonization of government programs. The program augmented government financing for social protection and supports a contributory protection scheme for injuries incurred on the job, offering protection to a wider population.

Source: Asian Development Bank.

Empowering women will catalyze transformative climate action. Effective response to climate challenges critically depends on empowered women. ADB will build on and scale up existing efforts to deliver gender-responsive and transformational climate action in DMCs. It will support capacity development and skill training, in part through a regional approach, targeting green jobs, entrepreneurship, and improved access to information, affordable technology, and finance for women to pursue climate action.

As climate change poses a critical risk to human health outcomes, it is essential to invest in inclusive and green health systems that are fit for a changing climate. Climate change is undermining significant gains made over the past few decades in global health in terms of health outcomes, air pollution, reproductive health, and other domains. Climate financing in health is deficient for lack of demand from sovereign clients and of capacity and tools to design transformative climate action for the sector. ADB will support DMC efforts to seize post-pandemic recovery opportunities to invest in green, resilient, and inclusive health systems. ADB will invest in efficient, low-carbon health-care facilities, equipment, operations, and supply chains, importantly ensuring a strong health-care supply chain that includes viable low-carbon cold chains for delivering medicine. Taking a systematic approach, the ADB package will encompass capacity building, policy, and financial support for interventions that address all core building blocks of a health-care system: leadership and governance, a trained workforce, information systems, essential medical products and technologies, service delivery, and financing.

Climate action must be embedded into education systems. It is critical that education sector plans and policies consider climate change, disaster risk, and environmental protection. School infrastructure needs to be built or renovated to be climate-smart and thus ensure a protective, healthy, and inclusive learning environment for all students while minimizing environmental footprints. As the low-carbon and climate-resilient transition will transform industries, new skills must be taught. ADB will increase support for human capital development, nurturing expertise and skills to enable the adoption of new climate-smart technologies and processes. It will invest in climate-smart educational facilities and the inclusion of climate-smart knowledge and technical skills in technical and vocational education and training. ADB will enhance support for DMC efforts to integrate climate-smart competencies—notably system thinking and recognizing sustainability as a core value—into curricula at all levels of education including teachers' training. This entails developing programs that integrate youth into the market for green jobs and promoting behavioral change toward sustainable lifestyles and consumption.

4.3 Climate-smart infrastructure

Investment in infrastructure today must be low carbon and climate resilient. Millions of people in the region, especially in low- and middle-income countries, lack access to basic services such as affordable clean energy and transportation, clean water, and modern sanitation. Climate change magnifies this challenge. As 75% of the infrastructure needed by 2050 has yet to be constructed,[25] infrastructure investment must be guided by principles for planning, design, delivery, and management that are low-carbon, climate and disaster resilient, inclusive, and just. ADB will continue to invest in climate-smart infrastructure to deliver basic services and will scale up investment in newer types of climate-smart infrastructure that incorporate the circular economy and resource efficiency. Actions will encompass expanding and improving key infrastructure in all sectors, and particularly in energy, cross-border connectivity, transport, water, and urban infrastructure (Box 17). To avoid higher emissions, they will promote decarbonization by switching from fossil fuels to renewable energy, using low-carbon materials, and improving energy efficiency, among other climate-smart measures.

Box 17: Asia and the Pacific Water Resilience Initiative

ADB launched the Asia and Pacific Water Resilience Initiative in 2022 with two main objectives:

(i) Mobilize at least $200 million in grant and technical assistance from internal sources and external partners by 2026 to support water resilience, including the new $20 million Water Resilience Trust Fund established in January 2023, and leverage $10 billion in climate finance for the water sector from ADB's own resources by 2030.

(ii) Build capacity and share knowledge, tools, and solutions on resilience through the Asia Pacific Water Resilience Hub, to empower water entities on the ground.

Source: Asian Development Bank.

Energy, transport, and urban infrastructure are large and rising sources of GHG emissions in Asia and the Pacific. For transformational change to decarbonize at scale, infrastructure investments need to be planned and designed in an integrated manner. Electricity and heat production, transport, residential buildings, and commercial and public services collectively accounted in 2020 for nearly 70% of energy-related emissions in Asia and the Pacific.[26] Wastewater treatment processes produce some of the most potent GHGs, notably nitrous oxide and methane. Heavy industry to produce steel, cement, aluminum, chemicals, plastics, and metals are—like mining, aviation, and heavy-duty transport—highly energy intensive. ADB will enhance support for DMC responses to emerging needs in the changing energy landscape to ensure that investments in long-lived infrastructure are climate-smart, using sustainable construction materials for infrastructure that will be environmentally and economically sustainable over the long term. Investment in urban infrastructure provides especially extensive opportunities to pursue mitigation and adaptation simultaneously and thus achieve resilience.

The energy sector has a critical role to play in decarbonizing the region. DMCs still face important challenges to ensuring universal energy access, safeguarding energy security, improving energy sector governance, and enhancing sustainability. While many DMCs have made significant progress in these areas, they need continued support to consolidate achievements and address emerging challenges and opportunities. ADB will facilitate DMC transitions to sustainable, lower-carbon, and resilient energy systems, in particular by accelerating the deployment of renewable energy and energy efficiency across power, heating, and cooling systems, especially in energy-intensive industries and buildings, and by making energy infrastructure climate resilient. ADB will continue to support initiatives to accelerate

---

[25] The New Climate Economy. 2016. *The Sustainable Infrastructure Imperative*.
[26] ADB calculation based on International Energy Agency. 2022. *Greenhouse Gas Emissions from Energy*.

the retirement of coal-fired power plants and pursue the strategic decarbonization of power generation, buildings, and industry. Focus will continue to be on projects that accelerate the deployment of renewable energy, energy efficiency, and energy storage solutions at scale, and that develop an integrated regional market for power trade that facilitates the maximized utilization of renewable power sources in the region (footnote 11). ADB will support financial intermediaries and the private sector with finance for renewable-energy and energy-efficiency projects pursued by small and medium-sized enterprises (Box 18).

Box 18: Energy sector solutions

National Solar Park Project in Cambodia. ADB helped the Government of Cambodia develop its largest utility-scale solar photovoltaic (PV) project in the country through a public–private partnership approach, enabling the lowest ever solar PV tariff in Southeast Asia. Project success prompted ADB to support the development in Cambodia of up to 2 gigawatts of additional solar PV combined with battery storage.

Energy efficiency in India. ADB provided a $200 million loan and a $13 million grant to establish a revolving fund for energy-efficiency to finance light-emitting diode (LED) streetlights, LED bulbs for buildings, ceiling fans, electric vehicles, and charging stations through a public energy service company.

Pacific Renewable Energy Investment Facility. This 10-year facility was designed to take a programmatic approach to implementing reform and small renewable energy projects across 11 small Pacific island countries. It allows small projects to be processed more quickly and with lower transaction costs, with project processing streamlined by the ADB Board of Directors' delegating authority to the President to approve qualifying projects with cumulative ADB financing up to $200 million. The facility supports renewable energy, battery energy storage, and a transmission and distribution grid.

Source: Asian Development Bank.

Urgent action is required to turn around transport in Asia and the Pacific, which is the fastest-growing source of carbon emissions globally. Transport is one of the most emission-intensive sectors in Asia and the Pacific, necessitating aggressive measures to advance climate adaptation and curtail emissions. As economic development and urbanization continue, DMCs have high demand for transport projects to complete core transport infrastructure or enhance efficiency and management. Immense scope exists to scale up climate-smart transport investment. ADB will strengthen support to decarbonize transport through an avoid–shift–improve approach that favors low-carbon multimodal transport systems that integrate electric rail, e-vehicles, and associated charging infrastructure with safe nonmotorized transport. Prioritized action will ensure the long-term viability of transport infrastructure.

ADB will enhance investment in climate-smart infrastructure and supply chains in sectors requiring little infrastructure. Particular sectors are agriculture and natural resources, tourism, education, public health, and financial services. Investment will support undisrupted access to services and labor to enhance the quality of life and make the private sector more competitive.

4.4 Biodiversity, agrifood systems, and nature-based climate solutions

Conserving biodiversity plays a critical role in the fight against climate change. Healthy ecosystems are strongly interlinked and have great potential to mitigate and adapt to climate change. Over half of global gross domestic product, nearly $58 trillion, is moderately or highly dependent on nature, including water, forest, and marine resources.[27] Governments and the private sector are becoming ever more aware of the need to understand risks posed by biodiversity loss to the economy and society, and of the need to conserve and sustainably use biodiversity and natural resources. However, biodiversity continues to be lost at an alarming rate. Over 1 million species are currently at risk of extinction, and terrestrial and marine ecosystems are deteriorating more quickly than ever.[28] In 2021 alone, 3.75 million hectares of tropical forests were cleared, creating emissions equal to those from annual fossil fuel use in India that year.[29] The human-induced drivers of climate change and biodiversity loss perversely drive one another. Half of the human-made global carbon emissions are absorbed by land-based and marine ecosystems. While oceans, forests, mangroves, and peatland are natural carbon sinks, biodiversity loss and degraded land and water undermine ecosystem function and services that mitigate climate change by absorbing carbon and enhance adaptation and climate resilience. The impacts of climate change on biodiversity are rapidly becoming more evident, as forest fires around the globe in 2022 and 2023 have demonstrated. The landmark approval of the Kunming–Montreal Global Biodiversity Framework shows there is now a global consensus on the need "to take urgent action to halt and reverse biodiversity loss to put nature on a path to recovery."[30] ADB will contribute to achieving framework goals and address the issue of biodiversity loss through its updated safeguard policy and by supporting nature-positive DMC initiatives.[31] The ADB safeguard policy will now include environmental and social standards dedicated to biodiversity conservation and sustainable natural resource management, as well as attention to climate change.

Climate objectives are served by mainstreaming conservation and the sustainable use of biodiversity and growing a nature-positive portfolio. ADB recognizes that promoting healthy and resilient ecosystems requires integrated approaches beyond traditional approaches to biodiversity conservation. Holistic economic, social, and environmental diagnosis will assess ecosystem functions and any services affected by projects.[32] This approach will ensure that biodiversity co-benefits delivered for climate change mitigation, adaptation, and resilience are fully accounted for and better reflected in projects. It will facilitate further complementarity and mainstreaming of nature-based solutions into traditional linear infrastructure projects for roads, railways, bridges, and tunnels. It will also present the economic case for championing ecosystem restoration and regenerative agriculture and growing a more dedicated nature-positive portfolio. In 2021, ADB signed the MDB joint nature statement,[33] reinforcing its ambition to grow its portfolio of nature initiatives toward delivering on its climate targets. Flagship efforts like the Regional Flyway Initiative[34] and Healthy Oceans Program[35] are some initial efforts with the scale necessary for significant impact. Recognizing a huge funding gap for nature,[36] ADB plans to innovate finance solutions that unlock capital for DMCs and allow them to rapidly scale up nature-positive projects and initiatives. The vision is that these innovations and nature-based solutions will come to occupy a significant proportion of the climate portfolio.

---

[27] World Economic Forum. 2023. *Why Measuring the Economic Value of Ecosystems Is Important*.
[28] Intergovernmental Science-Policy Platform on Biodiversity and Ecosystem Services. 2019. *Global Assessment Report on Biodiversity and Ecosystem Services*.
[29] Global Forest Watch. 2022. *Global Forest Watch Forest Loss Remained Stubbornly High in 2021*.
[30] UN Convention on Biological Diversity. 2022. *Kunming–Montreal Global Biodiversity Framework*.
[31] ADB. 2023. *Draft Environmental and Social Framework*.
[32] P. Dasgupta. 2021. *The Economics of Biodiversity: The Dasgupta Review*.
[33] ADB. 2021. *ADB, Multilateral Banks Commit to Mainstreaming Nature at COP26*. News release. 2 November.
[34] ADB. 2022. *Regional Flyway Initiative: Investing in the East Asian–Australasian Flyway for Nature and People*.
[35] ADB. 2022. *ADB Healthy Oceans Implementation Plan 2022–2024*.
[36] Paulson Institute. 2020. *Financing Nature: Closing the Global Biodiversity Financing Gap*.

Agriculture urgently needs transformation to meet global climate objectives while providing food security. Agrifood systems contribute almost a third of global GHG emissions.[37] Livestock and rice are major emitters of methane, the second-most-abundant GHG. Agrochemical production, agrifood processing, and supply chain logistics are highly energy intensive. Moreover, feeding a growing population with increasingly diverse food and nutrition needs and preferences threatens to push up GHG emissions. Agrifood systems in the region are dominated by smallholder farmers, who are among the people most affected by climate change. While over $200 billion is needed every year to achieve the climate transition in agrifood systems, only $28.5 billion in climate finance was mobilized for the sector in 2019–2020.[38] It is a global imperative to multiply these investments by at least sevenfold. ADB is committed to doing its part and announced in September 2022 plans to provide at least $14 billion in 2022–2025 to support short-term responses to food security challenges and to address over the longer term climate change and biodiversity loss.

Future ADB agriculture investments will be climate-smart, proactively harnessing opportunities for high productivity and a just transition. ADB investments have focused on adaptation with investment in water resources, irrigation and flood risk management, and climate-smart agribusiness value chains. Mitigation investment in agrifood systems has been smaller, though avenues are expanding for investment in renewable energy, energy efficiency, carbon sequestration, bio-circularity, stemming food waste, and reducing carbon intensity along value chains. Ample opportunity exists for nature-based land and marine resource management to mitigate climate change. ADB will support climate-smart agrifood systems and nature-based climate solutions in high-emission areas such as livestock and rice, fertilizer production and application, and agri-processing and logistics, as well as for a just transition. It will use sovereign investment, advocate policy to repurpose public subsidies, and mobilize investment by the private sector and through finance intermediaries. By leveraging green and blue finance, commercial cofinance, and donor funds, ADB can generate new cash flow into agrifood systems and rural communities to incentivize the adoption of low-carbon and climate-resilient activities at scale.

Nature provides viable solutions for climate resilience through adaptation and mitigation, in particular carbon storage. Nature-based climate solutions are critical to implementing the Kunming–Montreal Global Biodiversity Framework and thus halting and reversing biodiversity loss. Asia and the Pacific have great potential to employ cost-effective nature-based climate solutions. Recent analysis identifies how nature-based climate solutions can address climate risk at scale, often more cost-effectively and flexibly than conventional alternatives, and offer significant co-benefits to local communities, particularly to such vulnerable populations as women, indigenous peoples, and youth.[39] Nature-based climate solutions offer significant social, environmental, cultural, and economic benefits. They contribute to rural development, sustainable livelihoods, and food security by adopting a complete-food-chain approach to agrifood system transformation that, among other benefits, boosts the productivity and sustainability of agrifood systems while enhancing carbon storage.[40] In urban areas, nature-based climate solutions can prevent flooding while creating green spaces to make cities more livable. They can advance gender equality by promoting economic empowerment and providing women with income-generating opportunities. Securing the rights of indigenous peoples to their land and resources, and harnessing their local knowledge, are among the most effective ways to protect and restore fragile ecosystems.[41] Building on existing initiatives for nature-based climate solutions, ADB will significantly strengthen its own capacity in this area through innovative funding and knowledge solutions able to advance the agenda (Box 19).

---

[37] Food and Agriculture Organization. 2021. *Greenhouse Gas Emissions from Agrifood Systems: Global, Regional and Country Trends, 2000–2020*.
[38] Climate Policy Initiative. 2023. *Landscape of Climate Finance for Agrifood Systems*.
[39] ADB. 2022. *Integrating Nature-based Solutions for Climate Change Adaptation and Disaster Risk Management: A Practitioner's Guide*.
[40] A complete-food-chain approach considers land use, storage, transport, packaging, processing, retail, and consumption, some components of which can be improved by adopting nature-based climate solutions.
[41] International Land Coalition. 2021. *The Role of Local Communities and Indigenous Peoples in Asia in Ecosystem Restoration and Conservation*.

> **Box 19: Examples of ADB initiatives on nature-based climate solutions**
>
> **Regional Flyway Initiative.** This is a partnership to protect, restore, and sustainably manage a network of threatened natural wetlands—mangrove forests, peatland, marshes, tidal mudflats, and coral atolls—along the East Asian–Australasian Flyway. Richly biodiverse wetlands provide vital ecosystem services to nearly 200 million people, sustaining agriculture, fisheries, and tourism. More than 50 million migratory waterbirds of more than 210 species depend on them, as do many other animal and plant species. These ecosystems are crucial to combating climate change as they sequester significant greenhouse gas emissions and enhance climate resilience.
>
> **Natural Capital Hub.** This is a platform to incubate, accelerate, and scale up nature-based solutions to protect ecosystem services and address climate change across sectors. The lab has three key focus areas: (i) natural resource management for eco-tourism, sustainable forestry, wetland protection, sustainable land management, animal health, and welfare protection; (ii) climate-resilient agriculture that features rainwater harvesting, water reuse systems, flood management, modern irrigation, and carbon sequestration; and (iii) sustainable food value chains generated through digitalization, regenerative farming, sustainable protein solutions, advanced greenhouse farming, small market solutions, and vertical farming. Hub activities measure and valuate natural capital, connect science with policy and regulatory frameworks around nature, design and develop sustainable financing and payment mechanisms, and produce and share knowledge through partnerships.
>
> **Climate-Resilient Community-Based Agroforestry Value Chain Project.** This Indonesian project is ADB's first direct investment in a private forestry and timber company. It supports the integration of canopy-level forestry with smallholder farms, creating multistory agroforestry systems that provide farmers with diverse income streams. Multitier agroforestry has significant potential to advance climate adaptation and mitigation, biodiversity protection, rural livelihoods, and food security.
>
> Source: Asian Development Bank.

ADB recognizes that carbon finance can incentivize finance for nature-based climate solutions. Carbon markets can make nature-based climate solutions more financially viable by enhancing return on investment through the sale of carbon credits. Investors gain confidence as tightened monitoring, reporting, and verification standards improve transparency. To enable nature-based climate solutions, ADB will offer TA, build capacity, and mobilize carbon finance.

4.5 Green and blue climate finance

ADB will help DMCs scale up climate finance in alignment with the Paris Agreement. It will engage DMCs in dialogue on policy direction and institutional strengthening, to ensure that DMC finance systems can realize the opportunities presented by climate change and manage the risks. ADB is well positioned to assist financial supervisors, regulators, and policy makers in designing and implementing actions that will enable and facilitate climate-positive development. ADB will support DMCs' transition to net-zero and climate-resilient economies. ADB will help them manage climate risk to their finance systems, support the development of their transition finance, and scale up climate finance by mobilizing the private sector.

Central banks and standard-setting bodies should integrate environment and climate change into their policy frameworks. ADB will work with these bodies to develop regulatory and supervisory approaches that address biodiversity and climate risks amplified by and imposed on finance systems. Topics include environmental risks from projects, green monetary policy, asset vulnerability to climate change, and greening micro- and macroprudential frameworks. ADB will increasingly use policy-based instruments and TA to integrate environmental and climate considerations into policy frameworks, building capacity in regulators and standard-setters to compile local taxonomies for merging with the international framework.[42]

Finance institutions need to manage risks in the low-carbon and climate-resilient transition and to recognize opportunities. Finance intermediaries must have the means to increase lending in favor of climate-smart opportunities and the transition. ADB will provide support to establish and scale up dedicated national or regional green investment banks, funds, and transition finance vehicles, as well as green funding windows within national development finance institutions. It will complement this with TA to help financial institutions understand and manage their exposure to transition and physical risks. Box 20 briefly describes an example of ADB support for finance that combines climate action and the Sustainable Development Goals.[43]

Box 20: Example of support for climate and Sustainable Development Goal finance

ADB supports the Sustainable Development Goals Indonesia One—Green Finance Facility with a $150 million loan to the Government of Indonesia for relending to PT Sarana Multi Infrastruktur, a state-owned infrastructure finance institution. The facility will finance projects that meet green, financial bankability, and leverage targets with the aim of catalyzing funds from private, institutional, and commercial sources. In addition to the loan, technical assistance is provided to enhance the firm's subproject pipeline and monitoring system, strengthen green and Sustainable Development Goal subproject pipelines and government capacity, and develop future phases and road maps for the facility.

Source: Asian Development Bank.

ADB helps establish and strengthen sustainable capital markets aligned with the Paris Agreement. Building on the Thailand Green Bond Project, ADB will expand its portfolio of green, blue, and other climate-labeled bonds and continue to support the establishment of local markets issuing local currency bonds and help banks issue their own green bonds (Box 21). This will include working with sovereign issuers as appropriate and developing more innovative products to accelerate the net-zero transition: sustainability-linked bonds and transition bonds guaranteed, for example, through the Credit Guarantee and Investment Facility of ADB's Asian Bonds Markets Initiative, and advisory services and tools to help clients develop, issue, and track thematic bonds. ADB will explore vehicles to leverage other investors' money, provide access to a wider investor base, and be an anchor investor in thematic bonds to scale up the market for labeled bonds across the region. Upstream TA will enhance the enabling environment for green capital markets, and additional downstream technical support will be offered to bond issuers.

---

[42] ADB will work with standard-setting bodies like the International Sustainability Standards Board (ISSB), formed by the trustees of the International Financial Reporting Standards (IFRS) Foundation and the International Organization of Securities Commissions. ISSB standards entail the General Requirements for Disclosures of Sustainability-Related Financial Information (IFRS S1), Climate-Related Disclosures (IFRS S2), and the Global Reporting Initiative (GRI), the global leader for impact reporting.

[43] Other examples are Credit Enhancement of Project Bonds in India, Creating Ecosystems for Green Local Currency Bonds for Infrastructure Development in ASEAN+3, and Deploying Solar Systems at Scale.

> **Box 21: Increasing leverage of national resources focused on climate investments**
>
> The Thailand Green Bond Project is an example of ADB support to help institutions tap local capital markets for climate investment. The project constructed and refinanced 16 solar power plants in Thailand with a combined capacity of 98.5 megawatts. The B.Grimm Group issued corporate bonds to finance these solar assets, and ADB subscribed for $155 million, subject to their being recognized as green bonds under the International Capital Markets Association's Green Bond Principles, which ADB facilitated. ADB assisted B.Grimm with its application to the Climate Bond Initiative for the bonds to be certified as climate bonds under its Climate Bond Standards. As these were the first bonds compliant with Green Bond Principles to be issued by an energy company, and the first bonds in Thailand certified by the Climate Bond Initiative, the project contributed to the development of the green bond market in Thailand and the region.
>
> Source: Asian Development Bank.

ADB will help DMCs achieve their climate ambitions with innovative finance and green digital technology. ADB will promote the development of green digital technology by, for example, encouraging green consumption through digital payment platforms and crowding in co-finance for new technology development. It will help DMCs expand the impact and scale of climate investment, build capacity in national finance systems for climate investment, leverage national resources for climate investment, and mobilize additional finance partnerships. ADB can leverage sovereign finance to develop facilities that catalyze private sector finance. Where possible, ADB can further reduce costs by tapping the Green Climate Fund and similar global initiatives. It may use incentives, cross-subsidized lending rates, or lengthened financing tenor, as with the Shandong Green Development Fund in the People's Republic of China (Box 22).

> **Box 22: Shandong Green Development Fund Project**
>
> The Shandong Green Development Fund Project pilots an innovative leveraging mechanism to catalyze private, institutional, and commercial capital for climate-positive infrastructure and business. The project supports a portfolio of mitigation and adaptation subprojects assessed against climate and financial eligibility criteria and able to contribute to the transition to low-carbon and climate-resilient development. The fund aims to leverage private, institutional, and commercial finance for climate-resilient subprojects by financing a portion of capital expenditure on selected subprojects for a capped period. This makes them bankable by addressing upfront project risks while promoting advanced technologies and an integrated approach to climate change. Catalytic fund amounts and financing terms are linked to climate criteria and performance, in line with the Green Climate Fund framework and investment criteria.
>
> Source: Asian Development Bank.

ADB will catalyze finance for smaller enterprises to develop the green and blue economy and support the transition to net zero. More than 90% of enterprises in the region are small and medium-sized enterprises (SMEs). They provide up to 70% of jobs and are central to the development of a low-carbon and climate-resilient economy. ADB will provide longer-tenor financing to banks to improve energy efficiency in SMEs and shrink their carbon footprint. It will expand financing and TA to help SMEs integrate into green and blue value chains and to strengthen the pipeline of bankable green and blue projects, notably under the Action Plan for Healthy Oceans and Sustainable Blue Economies (Box 23).

> **Box 23: Action Plan for Healthy Oceans and Sustainable Blue Economies**
>
> In 2019, ADB launched the Action Plan for Healthy Oceans and Sustainable Blue Economies to expand financing and technical assistance for ocean health and marine economy projects to $5 billion from 2019 to 2024. Healthy oceans absorb carbon, offer massive potential for marine renewable energy, sustain marine biodiversity, and provide food security and livelihoods to billions of people in Asia and the Pacific. The gap to finance Asia's sustainable blue economy is estimated at $5.5 trillion, of which some $2 trillion is for small and medium-sized enterprises (SMEs). ADB aims to support finance for SMEs in several ways: project development, investor matching, and facilitated access to regional programs such as the Blue Finance Accelerator and SME BlueImpact Asia. ADB is lengthening finance tenor for banks, notably the Bank of Qingdao in the People's Republic of China, through a blue loan for onlending and other support for marine environment protection and sustainable blue economies.
>
> Source: Asian Development Bank.

ADB will work with DMCs to expand green, blue, and transition finance. DMCs can be enabled to use fiscal policy instruments more extensively to achieve climate change mitigation and adaptation objectives. Currently weak public financial management systems are unable to monitor and report climate-related budgets and expenses, but fiscal policies have potential to address climate change. Carbon pricing can play a key role as part of a broader climate policy architecture to help DMCs achieve their NDCs cost effectively. ADB will support the adoption and strengthening of domestic carbon pricing policies for both emission trading systems and carbon taxes, as well as other green taxes and reform to fossil-fuel subsidies. This will strengthen policy incentives for low-emission development and raise public revenue. ADB will help DMCs mobilize additional green, blue, and transition finance through the budget, subsidies to state-owned enterprises for capital and operating expenditure, official development assistance, and international funds. Efforts should be made to catalyze all private sources of finance, especially institutional and retail investors, including banks, pension and insurance funds, private equity funds, and corporate social responsibility funds.

The flow of private and climate finance to subnational governments needs to increase. More than half of infrastructure in Asia is delivered by subnational entities, giving cities a central role in attracting private sector finance for green projects. ADB will work directly with subnational governments to mainstream resilience, improve creditworthiness, and leverage private sector participation through commercial borrowing, municipals bonds, and PPP, thereby making private finance for climate-resilient infrastructure more affordable (Box 24).

> **Box 24: Creating investable cities**
>
> ADB's Creating Investable Cities initiative helps cities coordinate their planning, funding, and financing efforts to address bottlenecks that impede the private- and climate-financing they need to meet their 2030 nationally determined contributions and achieve the Sustainable Development Goals. Launched at the World Cities Summit in 2022, the initiative helps leading cities in Georgia, India, Indonesia, Malaysia, Mongolia, and Viet Nam generate a pipeline of bankable projects aligned with the Paris Agreement on urban mobility, social housing, the circular economy, and waste management. It supports cities' efforts to improve their own-source revenue, creditworthiness, and access to private sector capital and efficient partnership, notably through municipal bonds, carbon finance, and public–private partnership.
>
> Source: Asian Development Bank.

ADB will explore opportunities presented by international carbon markets for the public and private sector. ADB aims to mobilize carbon finance to incentivize investment in low-carbon technologies through domestic, bilateral, and international carbon markets and provide technical, capacity-building, and knowledge support to DMCs. It will maximize opportunities for public and private entities to attract innovative carbon finance, earmarked by jurisdiction or sector, from compliance and voluntary carbon markets by pioneering transactions in them under Article 6 of the Paris Agreement. Further, it will provide TA to public and private entities to develop the knowledge and infrastructure needed to bring high-integrity carbon credits to market.

The insurance industry plays an important role in climate and disaster risk finance. ADB will advance countries' efforts to be better prepared and respond more quickly to climate and disaster shocks by promoting additional financial protection instruments and finance sector regulatory reform to reduce climate risk. ADB sovereign and private sector projects need to integrate climate risk screening using robust diagnostic and risk modeling techniques and management measures that support adaptation and resilience. The insurance industry has developed sophisticated, probabilistic multi-hazard climate and disaster risk models that support risk-informed decision making for both the private and the public sector. The models improve understanding of disaster risk today and in the future under various scenarios. They can be used to evaluate how much loss can be averted with what prevention measures, and to assess benefits derived from risk transfer to international insurance and capital markets, such as through disaster relief bonds (Box 25). ADB will explore actions to upskill climate risk modeling and develop probabilistic risk models as a public good for DMCs. Moreover, the insurance industry provides products to bolster food security; ensure shock-responsive social protection; de-risk investment; and manage emerging cybersecurity, pandemic, climate, disaster, conflict, and displacement risks. Their substantial asset base to cofinance environmental, social, and governance investment will be crowded in to mobilize private sector finance.

Box 25: Disaster relief or catastrophe bonds

Disaster relief bonds are an innovative way for ADB to support climate adaptation at the sovereign or regional level. They are a form of insurance-linked security that transfers disaster risk from a "sponsor" to "investors" on the capital market. They are not a debt instrument but a viable form of ex-ante disaster-risk financing that benefits from a new community of private sector capital, and they provide immediate post-disaster grant financing when a predefined parameter, such as tropical cyclone wind speed, is triggered.

Source: Asian Development Bank.

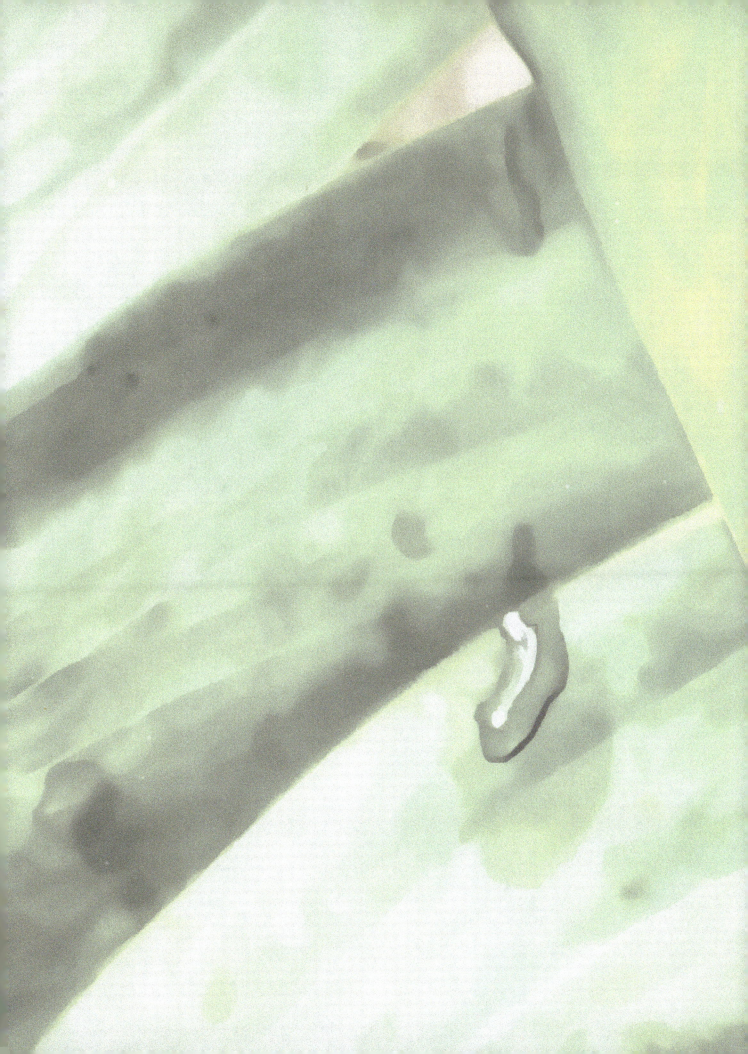

5 Implementing and monitoring climate action

The CCAP has implications for everyone in ADB. All departments and offices will be responsible for implementing it.

ADB must walk the talk by implementing climate action within the organization. Committed to reducing its own environmental impacts, ADB will (i) reduce its energy consumption; (ii) increasingly switch to renewable energy; (iii) reduce waste; (v) prioritize its procurement of products, works, and services from suppliers that have strong environmental and social-inclusiveness standards and are committed to sustainability; (vi) shrink its travel carbon footprint with sustainable transport, work from home, and selective business travel; and (vii) encourage staff engagement in sustainability initiatives. ADB will use carbon credits to offset residual GHG emissions from its operations at headquarters and in resident missions. Through its sustainability report, ADB will continue to report on its sustainability efforts as well as its own carbon emissions, energy use, and other environmental impacts.[44]

The Climate Action Coordination Committee (CACC) oversees implementation. The CACC is chaired by the managing director general and includes as members the heads of relevant departments, with the staff from the Strategy, Policy, and Partnerships Department and the Climate Change and Sustainable Development Department serving as the CACC secretariat. The CACC oversees implementation of the CCAP and meets every quarter. It may agree to change or update climate actions (Appendixes 1 and 2) as necessary to ensure continued relevance. The role of the CACC in overseeing the implementation of the CCAP will be reassessed at the CCAP midterm review.

The Climate Change and Disaster Risk Management (CCDRM) Advisory Group coordinates implementation and reports to the CACC. The CCDRM Advisory Group is co-chaired by the director for climate change and the head of disaster risk management and includes members from all departments involved in implementing the CCAP. The CCDRM advisory group meets every quarter. The role of the CCDRM advisory group will be reassessed at the CCAP midterm review.

The Climate Change, Resilience, and Environment Cluster (CCRE) has been established as part of the reorganization. The CCRE climate experts are strategically positioned across the organization and provide comprehensive support for the implementation of the CCAP. A CCAP coordinator position will be established in CCRE to provide coordination and monitoring based on specific terms of references. Staff will report on progress in implementing the CCAP and may raise any issues or concerns with the CCDRM Advisory Group as and when needed. An annual progress report will be prepared and presented to the ADB Board of Directors for information. A midterm review of the CCAP is proposed in 2026 for presentation as a report to senior management and shared for information with the ADB Board of Directors.

The CCDRM community of practice and focused working groups will support implementation. The CCDRM community of practice will welcome staff interested in sharing knowledge and expertise to implement the climate agenda. Focused working groups will be established for key CCAP deliverables. Each of the working groups will develop work plans for their deliverables, and group work plans will be reflected in individual work plans.

---

[44] ADB. 2022. *Asian Development Bank Sustainability Report 2022*. In 2021, ADB elected to support the Task Force on Climate-Related Financial Disclosures (TCFD) and published the TCFD-aligned report *Climate-Related Financials Disclosures 2021*. Since then, the major climate standards including TCFD have consolidated under the International Financial Reporting Standards Foundation (IFRS) of the International Sustainability Standards Board (ISSB). In June 2023, the ISSB published its sustainability and climate-related disclosures standards, termed IFRS S1 and S2.

ADB will bring climate experts closer to clients. ADB recognizes the need to move closer to clients and has led the way by increasing its presence through outposting and the strategic placement of climate change specialists in resident missions to guide climate dialogue with clients and development partners, support diagnostics, and facilitate pipeline development.[45] ADB representative offices will strengthen their strategic involvement to leverage climate partnerships with developed member economies, the private sector, and civil society.

ADB will invest in people by upskilling staff for climate action across the organization. Climate ambitions can be achieved only if all staff exhibit climate stewardship. ADB will increase its investment in leadership, learning, and skill development to enable staff to develop impactful climate-informed operations. It will enhance accountability for climate action by including these responsibilities as appropriate in staff job descriptions and departmental work plans. A capacity-development initiative for staff will span basic climate awareness and technical training to deepen climate knowledge as a complement to their areas of expertise. Senior management will be trained to lead ADB's climate shift. Upskilling will be necessary to strengthen collaboration, change-management, and engagement with clients and civil society. Behavioral indicators related to the application of ADB values regarding client-centricity, trustworthiness, and transformation will be included in staff day-to-day transactions and operations.

ADB will assess workforce and skill requirements. It will continue to analyze its workforce to ensure that it has the human resources and skills to deliver the CCAP. From 2021 to June 2023, ADB increased staffing for climate change from 35 to 95, including sector experts with climate change knowledge, sponsor-funded positions through the Workforce Rebalancing Framework, and repurposed staff positions to mainstream climate change in project processing and implementation. The number of staff in the climate change job family will increase to support the surge in climate action across ADB and to mainstream climate capacity and positions across the organization. ADB will further identify climate experts across sectors and regions and mobilize them for embedding in processing teams, including those with private sector experience. This will empower project teams themselves to shape project design and implementation for climate action, enabling more agile and speedy processing and maximum impact.

Climate action will be integrated into ADB's work program and budget framework (WPBF). The WPBF defines parameters and main thrusts for ADB operations to a 3-year planning horizon. This annual process reports on how proposed programs, projects, TA, and corporate initiatives align with ADB priorities. The WPBF exercise will ensure that engagements align qualitatively and quantitatively, over the long and short term, with ADB's climate finance ambition and key climate targets. The WPBF will be prepared in line with programming priorities, especially ADB's climate financing ambition.

Improved planning, monitoring, and evaluation will boost climate outcomes. ADB business processes have been streamlined for more effective and efficient project design and management, achieved by strengthening data management, feedback loops, and process monitoring. Ongoing refinement to the application of international climate accounting standards to improve data capture and consistency will be complemented by refinement to the application of carbon metrics. These assessments will support frameworks to measure progress toward development objectives.

ADB will manage toward climate results. It will continue to use key performance indicators in its CRF to manage toward meaningful climate results and report progress in its annual development effectiveness review. Climate performance indicators will be cascaded into the annual workplans of departments and offices to ensure that staff work together toward climate action priorities alongside other corporate priorities. Following the midterm review of Strategy 2030, the CRF will be updated to reflect ADB climate targets and ways of working aligned with the CCAP and the climate shift under the ADB new operating model.

---

[45] In the Pacific, a different operational model will be required, as most Pacific DMCs have small portfolios that cannot support a fully staffed resident mission. This model features Pacific country offices, which have deepened in-country links in the region and served as extensions of the two regional offices and ADB headquarters. ADB will continue to leverage Pacific country offices for in-country policy dialogue, donor coordination, project and TA development and implementation, and local engagement with civil society and nongovernmental organizations.

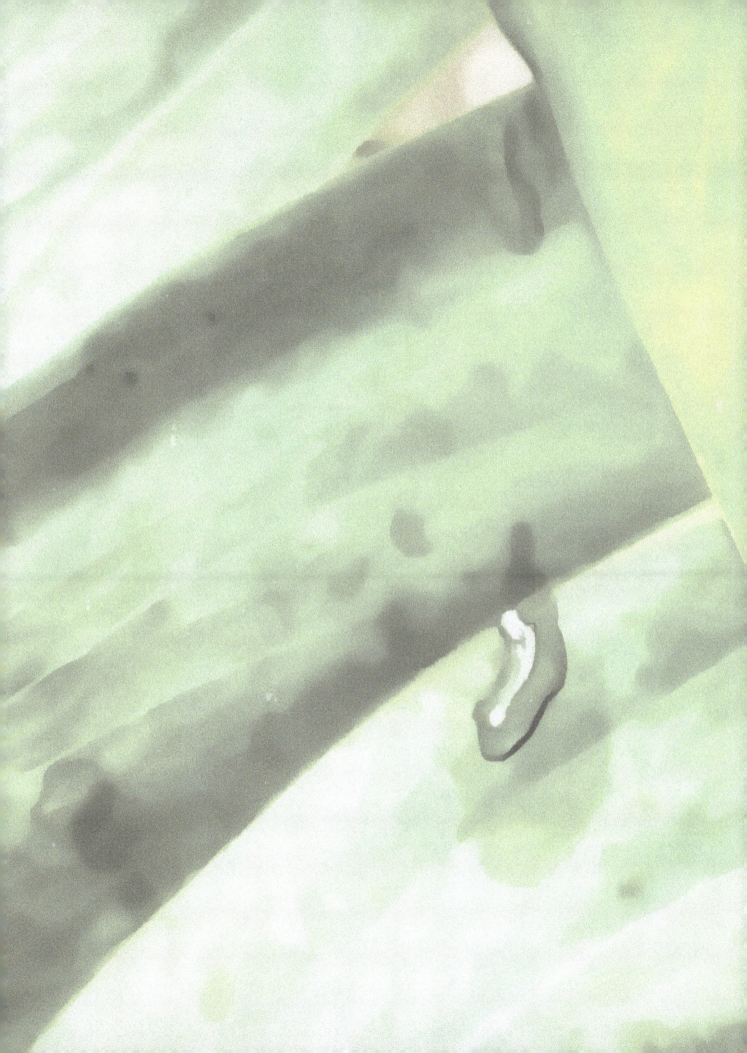

Appendixes

Appendix 1: List of climate actions

☐ Highlighted actions will be priorities for reporting to the Asian Development Bank (ADB) Board of Directors.

Action		Target Date	Responsibility
A.	**Strengthen partnerships for resource mobilization and efficient partner coordination.**		
A.1.	**Review and strengthen climate partnership structures.**		
	1. **Review and firm up ADBs climate partnership structures and approaches.** This includes climate-related knowledge and financing partnership arrangements that may need to be strengthened and updated.	31 Dec 2024	SPD, SG, CCSD
A.2.	**Establish new and strengthen existing collaboration with partners.**		
	1. **Support country climate development platforms and explore financing solutions.** Develop a country climate development platform in partnership with the Government of Bangladesh and other development partners. Establish the Nepal Green and Resilience Financing Facility in partnership with the Government of Nepal to create innovative financing solutions at scale at the country level. Both initiatives will inform ADB's broader approach to partner coordination on climate action and options to mobilize climate finance.	31 Dec 2024	SARD RDs
	2. **Establish the Climate and Health Initiative as a partnership facility.** In coordination with the Group of Twenty and the World Health Organization, establish the Climate and Health Initiative as a partnership facility dedicated to support climate-resilient and low-carbon health-care systems.	31 Dec 2023	SG-HSD[a]
	3. **Deepen climate collaboration with CSOs.** Deepen collaboration with CSOs through TA to help them raise awareness in local communities about climate-related issues. Set a clear plan to engage stakeholders in ADB climate initiatives. Establish a CSO-led seminar series for knowledge sharing and explore the feasibility of a CSO knowledge base.	31 Dec 2024	CCSD
	4. **Develop climate collaboration with CAREC through a climate vision.** The CAREC Climate Change Vision will provide a systematic and strategic regional approach to advance the climate agenda in the region. It will (i) serve as a guiding framework to reaffirm CAREC's focus on climate change as a crosscutting strategic theme, (ii) establish priorities for the CAREC program, (iii) integrate climate aspects into CAREC operational clusters, and (iv) outline opportunities for engagement on climate change with development partners including the CAREC Institute.	31 Dec 2023	CWRD
	5. **Organize an inter-subregional climate and trade knowledge forum.** Advocate through the forum greater integration of climate considerations into the regional cooperation and integration agenda. The forum will explore how to (i) decarbonize trade and supply chains, (ii) promote and support knowledge sharing among subregional programs in regional cooperation and integration that are relevant to climate change and trade activities, and (iii) identify approaches for innovative ADB lending operations with integrated solutions for climate change and trade.	31 Dec 2025	CCSD

continued on next page

Table continued

Action		Target Date	Responsibility
B.	**Upscale climate investment and its impact.**		
B.1.	**Incentivize climate investments.**		
	1. **Assess new approaches to incentivizing climate investments.** As part of the Strategy 2030 midterm review, and the update to the Concessional Assistance Policy for the ADF 14 period, and in consultation with ADF donors, assess options to expand access to concessional resources to incentivize high-impact and transformative national and regional climate projects. Options include (i) increasing the volume of concessional ordinary capital resources under the new capital adequacy framework and allocating a portion of this for climate projects, (ii) exploring the provision of more concessional terms for ordinary capital resources for climate projects, and (iii) examining barriers to subnational entities' access to climate financing. Relevant lending policy papers will be adjusted accordingly for Board consideration as needed.	31 Mar 2024	SPD
	2. **Prepare a climate categorization system for projects and develop staff guidance.** Develop a climate categorization system with incentives to allow differential access to concessional financial resources, streamlined business processes, and new modalities for projects and programs with highly beneficial climate impact and potential to change countries' development trajectories.	30 Jun 2024	CCSD, SPD
	3. **Assess a potential pilot for climate-resilient debt clauses.** Consider introducing climate-resilient debt clauses, initially as a pilot for small island developing states, possibly in collaboration with other development partners.	31 Mar 2024	SPD
B.2.	**Expand opportunities for climate finance.**		
	1. **Develop the Private Sector Climate Ambition Plan.** Identify opportunities to originate and mobilize more climate finance and consider approaches to identify regulatory barriers confronting the private sector. This can inform midstream, upstream, knowledge, and partnership activities across ADB. The Private Sector Climate Ambition Plan will look across sectors—energy, transport, agriculture and land use, industry, manufacturing, construction, real estate and green buildings, education, and health care—to find opportunities economy-wide to support decarbonization and climate resilience. It will facilitate a strategic approach to identifying potential instruments for climate finance investment, determining risk appetite, assessing the commercial readiness of different technologies and solutions across DMCs, and generating opportunities to cross-fertilize good climate finance models across ADB financing channels. This will include mapping private sector climate finance opportunities against the modalities to be undertaken.	31 Jul 2024	PSOD
	2. **Mobilize climate finance through sustainability-linked loans and bonds.** Prepare operational guidelines for processing and implementing sustainability-linked loans and bonds, thereby expanding ADB product offerings to address the urgent need to scale up climate finance.	31 Mar 2024	PSOD
	3. **Develop a debt-for-nature swap framework to support climate action.** Identify options for debt-for-nature swaps in suitable DMCs by introducing dedicated resource allocation and business process improvements.	31 Dec 2024	SG

continued on next page

Table continued

Action		Target Date	Responsibility
	4. **Support deep-tier supply chain finance for the Trade and Supply Chain Finance Program.** Contribute to the publication of a legal and technology framework to enable deep-tier supply chain finance to drive liquidity in the most underserved parts of global supply chains. Use deep-tier supply chain finance as a platform to motivate greater adoption of environmental, social, and governance standards and climate-friendly behavior in trade.	31 Mar 2024	PSOD
	5. **Support deep-tier supply chain finance for the Trade and Supply Chain Finance Program.** Contribute to the publication of a legal and technology framework to enable deep-tier supply chain finance to drive liquidity in the most underserved parts of global supply chains. Use deep-tier supply chain finance as a platform to motivate greater adoption of environmental, social, and governance standards and climate-friendly behavior in trade.	31 Mar 2024	PSOD
	6. **Develop a Central West Regional Climate Strategy.** The strategy aims to identify strategic entry points to mainstream and increase climate action in CWRD's operations. It will include (i) an assessments of countries climate contexts, (ii) an identification and prioritization of entry points for climate action in the Central and West Asia region, (iii) gender-sensitive climate country plans, and (iv) an action plan highlighting adaptation and mitigation pathways, capacity building, and communication approaches with targets, timelines, and resource requirements.	30 Jun 2024	CWRD
C.	**Strengthen ADB internal knowledge management and research.**		
C.1.	**Generate and manage climate knowledge for better climate solutions.**		
	1. **Develop a climate knowledge management plan.** Develop a knowledge management plan for the climate change group with a focus on enhancing learning from project design and implementation through case studies, training, and other forms of knowledge solutions, including through the enhanced use of impact evaluation underlying climate change interventions.	31 Dec 2024	CCSD, DOCK
	2. **Create a one-stop shop for innovative ADB climate work.** Establish a system to identify and support climate-smart pilot activities and report them in the Innovation Hub database to make it easy for staff, DMCs, and partners to learn about ADB projects and initiatives.	31 Jan 2024	DOCK
	3. **Develop a digital knowledge navigator for ADB climate knowledge.** Develop a taxonomy-informed information architecture linked with ADB's Electronic Document Record Management System. Map TA reports, climate projects, guidance, and training materials; roll out an expertise locator; and enhance technological solutions using artificial intelligence.	31 Jan 2025 (first phase)	DOCK, ITD
	4. **Enhance climate research and research collaboration.** Deepen and broaden expertise on climate change issues in DMCs and collaborate with leading research centers and other partners. Conduct and disseminate research on key climate policy issues, including impact evaluation of climate change interventions in the region. Outputs may include (i) three impact evaluation studies related to climate change, (ii) four studies at least touching on climate change, and (iii) collaboration with global climate partners to model initiatives for two or three DMCs.	31 Dec 2025	ERDI

continued on next page

Table continued

Action		Target Date	Responsibility
	5. **Launch a climate change flagship report.** Create a new ADB flagship publication on climate change that will provide in-depth analysis of climate policies, raise awareness of mitigation and adaptation efforts, and promote policy reform.	30 Nov 2024	ERDI
	6. **Develop guidelines on best practices for community-led participatory processes for climate initiatives.** Develop guidelines and knowledge for ADB and DMC staff on stakeholder engagement and participatory processes for inclusion and long-term sustainability in climate change initiatives.	31 Dec 2024	CCSD, RDs
C.2.	**Enhance capacity development on the climate agenda.**		
	1. **Complete and approve a detailed capacity development plan, identify relevant institutions, and establish partnerships to build staff capacity.** Develop capacity building and training options for staff, especially those in sector groups and regional departments. Investigate and identify possible external accreditation options on climate change for staff and DMC partners.	31 Dec 2024	BPMSD, CCSD
	2. **Enhance ADB staff capacity on gender-responsive climate action.** Develop a training module for ADB staff on gender mainstreaming in climate projects and train two cohorts of ADB staff.	31 Dec 2025	CCSD
	3. **Raise climate awareness and develop private sector capacity.** Work with selected corporate clients across infrastructure, financial intermediaries, agribusiness, social, industry, manufacturing, and real estate to develop corporate road maps for decarbonization and climate resilience. Mobilize TA to support this work. The exact targets and budget required will be determined in the Private Sector Climate Ambition Plan.	31 Jun 2025	PSOD
C.3.	**Strengthen climate knowledge dissemination and communication.**		
	1. **Develop and implement a climate communications plan.** Develop and implement external communication campaigns on the climate agenda, including climate-focused key messaging in business outreach and a climate survey helping to strengthen ADB's position as the climate bank for Asia and the Pacific. Develop and implement internal communications products on the roles of staff, consultants, and contractors and their accountability toward achieving ADB's mission as the regional climate bank.	30 Jun 2024	DOCK, CCSD
D.	**Upstream: Engage strategically for enhanced policy frameworks.**		
D.1.	**Strengthen support for DMC climate strategies and policies.**		
	1. **Support the preparation and implementation of nationally determined contributions and long-term strategies to enable the low-carbon transition.** Provide TA to help at least 20 DMCs with their nationally determined contributions and long-term strategies. Support linking them with national sector development plans, finance sector reforms, and other national development and economic policies.	31 Dec 2025	CCSD, RDs
	2. **Establish a just transition financing facility.** Establish a just transition financing facility through collaborative design to provide concessional resources for interventions in DMCs that ensure a just transition.	31 Dec 2025	CCSD

continued on next page

Table continued

Action		Target Date	Responsibility
	3. **Enhance the approach to sustainable investment in mountainous countries.** Secure resources to commence the implementation of the Hindu Kush Himalya Initiative in Bhutan and Nepal.	31 Dec 2023	CCSD, SARD
	4. **Enhance approaches to strengthen action for gender-responsive climate adaptation.** Develop gender-responsive approaches to managing heat stress. Provide TA to help DMCs develop gender-responsive heat action plans and increase knowledge, awareness, and support for DMC efforts to manage heat stress impacts through gender-responsive policies, planning, and locally led solutions.	31 Dec 2025	CCSD
D.2.	**Strengthen analytical frameworks.**		
	1. **Develop a climate assessment framework and carry out assessments in selected DMCs.** Strengthen upstream analysis by developing a climate assessment framework and by piloting it in selected DMCs in coordination with existing and ongoing work by other development partners to support the development and programming of country partnership strategies.	31 Dec 2024	CCSD, RDs
	2. **Establish GHG footprint analyses.** Analyze GHG footprints across sectors and industries to identify mitigation opportunities. Develop GHG footprint analyses in accordance with international standards on disclosure and reporting frameworks.	30 Jun 2024	SG, CCSD
	3. **Strengthen economic analysis for investments.** Enhance economic analysis to improve assessments of the costs, benefits, and risks of climate change and environmental externalities. Outputs may review existing guidance notes and prepare new ones on general or sector-specific economic analysis of climate investments and the valuation of ecosystem services and other co-benefits as well as costs. Improve the capacity of operational staff to conduct economic analysis of climate investments.	31 Dec 2025	ERDI
D.3.	**Strengthen climate-responsive financial systems in DMCs.**		
	1. **Support DMC alignment with international standards.** Engage with standard-setting bodies to help DMCs better address climate-related financial risks to the global financial system by (i) strengthening their regulation and supervision of banks and nonbank financial institutions to enhance financial stability, and (ii) building capacity to ensure that the financial sector has the knowledge and tools to measure and manage climate risks effectively.	31 Dec 2026	SG-FIN,[a] ORM, CTL, CCSD
	2. **Accelerate transition finance in DMCs.** Mainstream a transition finance framework in the operations of public and private finance institutions in DMCs and establish dedicated transition finance facilities to accelerate the net-zero transition in high-emitting industries.	30 Dec 2025	SG-FIN
	3. **Implement innovative climate financing mechanisms.** Help DMCs achieve their climate ambitions by using innovative financing mechanisms to close large financing gaps for climate action through the development and implementation of diverse innovative green financial approaches and instruments: green investment banks; green and blue bonds; social bonds; sustainability linked bonds; environment, social, and governance bonds; climate credit mechanisms; green and blue securitization; and Sustainable Development Goal bonds.	30 Dec 2026	SG-FIN

continued on next page

Table continued

Action		Target Date	Responsibility
E.	**Midstream: Embed climate action into core institutions and national systems.**		
E.1.	**Support climate investment planning in DMCs.**		
	1. **Pilot country climate investment plans supporting country partnership strategy implementation.** Pilot the development of climate investment plans for TA and lending operations in selected DMCs to support the implementation of country partnership strategies. Plans should span sovereign, private sector, and public–private partnership assistance, with targeted action to meet climate and development priorities, including nationally determined contributions and national adaptation plans.	31 Dec 2024	RDs
	2. **Enhance DMC capacity to integrate climate considerations into fiscal decision-making.** Develop TA to enhance the knowledge and skills of DMC officials through training, knowledge events, and the development of guidance notes about climate change, carbon pricing, fossil fuel subsidies, sustainable budgeting, domestic resource mobilization, and intergrating climate considerations into fiscal decision processes.	30 Oct 2024	SG-PSMG[a]
	3. **Strengthen institutions for developing private sector climate change projects.** Support the establishment or strengthening of about five institutions, such as public–private partnership centers, that can support the development of climate projects structured to enable efficient private sector participation.	31 Dec 2024	OMDP
	4. **Strengthen programmatic approaches to adaptation action in selected DMCs.** Scale up support for adaptation action in selected DMCs through programmatic approaches targeting the most vulnerable communities.	31 Dec 2026	CCSD, RDs
	5. **Establish a One ADB approach to helping DMCs develop enabling frameworks for private sector investment.** Establish an Interdepartmental task force to develop a One ADB approach to helping DMCs develop enabling frameworks for private sector investment.	31 Dec 2023 (taskforce established)	PSOD
	6. **Support DMCs with actions related to loss and damage.** Strengthen links between investments for climate adaptation and disaster risk management, including post-disaster response, recovery, and reconstruction, to support DMC recovery from climate-related loss and damage.	30 Oct 2024	CCSD, RDs
E.2.	**Integrate sustainable procurement considerations in the ADB procurement framework and DMC public procurement systems.**		
	1. **Assess country systems for sustainable procurement in each DMC.** Complete assessments in consultation with each DMC.	31 Dec 2024	PPFD, RDs
	2. **Develop a country support strategy for sustainable procurement.** Include recommended areas of support—procurement system diagnoses, policy action, institutional capacity building, or pilots—to better integrate sustainable procurement into the country system.	31 Dec 2025	PPFD, RDs
	3. **Pilot the integration of sustainable procurement practices into country public procurement systems and institutional frameworks.** Ensure alignment with countries' climate commitments and associated Sustainable Development Goals.	31 Dec 2026	PPFD, RDs

continued on next page

Table continued

Action		Target Date	Responsibility
	4. **Release ADB sustainable procurement guidance materials.** Incorporate sustainable procurement principles into strategic procurement planning and develop guidance materials for sustainable procurement and bidding documents, including evaluation criteria for climate change, carbon footprints, gender, and labor. Design selection evaluation criteria to incentivize consultants, contractors, and suppliers to do the same in their supply chain and in ADB-financed projects.	31 Mar 2024	PPFD
F.	**Downstream: Ensure high-quality operations and implementation.**		
F.1.	**Enhance private sector capacity for climate investment.**		
	1. **Enhance private sector capacity to work toward carbon neutrality.** A cluster TA program will be prepared to build capacity across the private sector, especially in financial intermediaries and hard-to-abate sectors. This will help the private sector move toward carbon neutrality.	31 Mar 2024 (TA approved)	PSOD
	2. **Prepare a directory of environmental, social, and governance services.** Develop and prepare a user-friendly online platform to provide information to small and medium-sized enterprises on environmental, social, and governance services and agencies.	30 Sep 2024	PSOD
	3. **Establish a carbon tracking and reporting framework.** Design and implement a framework and technical solution to track carbon emissions—and, eventually, other environmental, social, and governance data—across complex global supply chains in line with international financial reporting standards. Measure and report Scope 1, 2, and 3 emissions and assess compliance and noncompliance against selected standards or regulatory requirements to make supply chains more sustainable and help small and medium-sized suppliers maintain access to export markets.	31 Dec 2025	PSOD
	4. **Expand the environmental and social management system for the Trade and Supply Chain Finance Program.** The environmental and social management system strengthens environmental and social risk management for trade finance, implementing best practices aligned with ADB processes and procedures. Expand the deployment of this system to eight additional partner banks in 2023 and annually thereafter until the whole portfolio has access to it. The Trade and Supply Chain Finance Program aims to support the whole portfolio of DMC partner banks by 2030.	31 Dec 2030	PSOD
F.2.	**Improve climate related project due diligence.**		
	1. **Assess integrated digital analytic systems for aligning climate risk and Paris Agreement commitments.** Establish a digital analytic tool to better quantify and visualize climate and disaster risks, and assess and monitor Paris Agreement alignment. Integrate the system in ADB operations and make it available to DMCs.	30 Jun 2026	CCSD, ITD
	2. **Identify good practices for mainstreaming gender in climate change and disaster risk management projects.** Develop inclusive, gender-responsive, and participatory climate-focused planning processes supported by environmental governance and comprehensive planning. Catalyze transformative climate action by empowering women and young people.	30 Jun 2024	CCSD

continued on next page

Table continued

Action		Target Date	Responsibility
F.3.	Expand finance product offerings for climate investments.		
	1. Propose incentives for programmatic approaches that support low-carbon and climate-resilient development. Set up an internal working group to explore incentives for the use of programmatic approaches, including policy-based and results-based lending, to support DMC climate action.	31 Dec 2024	CCSD, SPD
	2. Further deploy One ADB action to scale up climate adaptation and mitigation efforts across the Pacific. Review opportunities to scale up differentiated approaches in the Pacific, including for safeguards and emerging issues in climate adaptation projects. Take stock of the use of differentiated procurement models under ADB's Procurement Policy (2017) and recommend further enhancements. Identify options to streamline client reporting documents to reduce the implementation burden while maintaining integrity. Assess staff capacity and TA resources to support diagnostics, project preparation, and on-the-ground implementation.	31 Dec 2024	PARD
	3. Operationalize the Climate Action Catalyst Fund. Operationalize the Climate Action Catalyst Fund to mobilize carbon finance and incentivize investments in low-carbon technologies and solutions, including those reducing GHG emissions with high global warming potential, through the purchase of mitigation outcomes or internationally transferred mitigation outcomes under Article 6 of the Paris Agreement.	31 Jan 2024	CCSD
	4. Support at least three DMCs through the Article 6 support TA facility. Partner with at least three DMCs on diagnostic studies to provide recommendations on how carbon pricing instruments can be used and embedded in national climate policy architecture, and to develop national frameworks toward a national climate policy for participating in international carbon markets.	31 Dec 2024	CCSD, OMDP
G.	Integrate low-carbon and climate-resilient solutions across operations.		
G.1.	Upscale technology adoption and enhanced climate solutions.		
	1. Establish and operationalize the ADB-Korea Climate Technology Hub. The hub will promote innovation and the adoption of technology for climate action.	31 Dec 2024	CCSD
	2. Strengthen planning and design support for low-carbon and climate-resilient urban development. Engage upstream with DMC counterparts beyond the national and city level. Further integrate urban planning to identify synergies offered by, for example, transit-oriented development. Promote participatory urban planning processes. Strengthen risk-informed land-use planning. Promote digital technology in urban planning, construction, and operation.	31 Dec 2030	SG-WUD[a]
	3. Support the development of climate-smart infrastructure design standards. Support the development of climate-smart infrastructure design standards and green building standards, and the regional adoption of energy-efficiency standards for key technologies.	31 Dec 2027	SG

continued on next page

Table continued

Action		Target Date	Responsibility
	4. **Scale up investment in and mobilize new types of transformation-enabling infrastructure.** Support and finance electric vehicle charging facilities, green hydrogen, renewable energy from battery-hybrid systems, infrastructure that promotes circular economy approaches, flood defense, low-carbon water production facilities, and digital infrastructure including early warning, early action systems, and social protection for disaster readiness.	31 Dec 2030	SG-ENE[a]
	5. **Establish a program to accelerate the transition to low-carbon transport.** Explore a new ADB-wide program to accelerate the low-carbon transition in transport. Design and expedite projects with work programs and upstream activities to meet cumulative 2030 climate-financing and result targets. Approve TA in the first quarter of 2024.	31 Mar 2024	SG-TRA[a]
	6. **Improve integrated water resource management in DMCs.** Help DMCs improve their integrated water resource management by strengthening policies and institutions and modernizing aging irrigation systems.	31 Dec 2030	SG-AFNR[a]
	7. **Promote financial inclusion.** Promote financial inclusion and green digital technologies by providing mitigation, transition, and adaption options to the most vulnerable people through access to various financial services: savings and remittance services to smooth consumption following drought or other crop failure; micro-loans to buy greener assets, fund asset conversion, and invest in climate-smart agriculture; and insurance to protect against yield fluctuations under climate change.	30 Dec 2026	SG-FIN
G.2.	**Upscale nature-based climate solutions in ADB operations.**		
	1. **Establish the Nature Solutions Finance Hub and the Nature Capital Fund.** Use the hub to support nature-based climate solutions by building on financial structuring models across policy outcomes and operations and thus generating a pipeline of bankable projects. The fund will crowd in investment to finance the pipeline developed by the hub and will explore public and private sources of finance and include blended-finance approaches to scale up private finance.	31 Mar 2025	CCSD, SG, PSOD, OMDP
	2. **Promote the financing of nature-based solutions.** Support selected DMCs in piloting public–private partnerships for coral reef financing and insurance to enable large-scale finance toward enhancing resilience in coastal businesses, communities, and livelihoods.	31 Dec 2024	SG-FIN
H.	**Implement and monitor climate action.**		
H.1.	**Update and monitor corporate climate targets and climate outcomes.**		
	1. **Update the corporate results framework.** Informed by the Strategy 2030 midterm review and the Climate Change Action Plan, update the corporate results framework to improve the monitoring and reporting of key result indicators to measure ADB operations' impact on climate adaptation and mitigation. Climate outcome indicators that are now being defined in cooperation with other multilateral development banks will inform the corporate results framework.	31 Dec 2024	SPD, CCSD

continued on next page

Table continued

Action		Target Date	Responsibility
	2. **Identify a consistent approach to tracking and communicating climate finance enabled and catalyzed by ADB.** Identify and develop a consistent approach to tracking and communicating what ADB achieves through its advisory, sovereign, and nonsovereign operations in terms of enabling private capital and catalyzing investment.	31 Mar 2024	SPD
	3. **Streamline the collection of climate finance data in ADB systems.** Streamline data collection in ADB systems, platforms, and documents to smooth its aggregation, reporting, and communication. Build staff capacity to apply the climate finance tracking approach and methodology. Assess digital tools to strengthen planning, tracking, and real time evaluation during project implementation to maximize operations' direct impact and catalyze further climate investment. Coordinate with other multilateral development banks on how to mainstream the approach in ADB.	30 Jun 2024	SPD, CCSD, CTL, ORM
	4. **Regularly assess and verify GHG emissions from ADB headquarters and field offices and offset them.** Operationalize the institutional climate secretariat established by CSD to address ADB GHG emissions from institutional operations, in line with Building Block 6 of the multilateral development bank framework, to align with the Paris Agreement and reach carbon neutrality in ADB headquarters and field offices.	31 Dec 2024	CSD
	5. **Enhance disclosure and reporting in line with changes to international standards and regulations.** Review internal processes, controls, and procedures to monitor, manage, and oversee climate risks. Review and develop frameworks to identify, assess, prioritize, and monitor material climate impacts and risks, including climate scenario analysis to inform the identification of risks.	30 Jun 2026	ORM, CTL
	6. **Release guidelines for assessing and reporting the carbon footprint of the ADB project portfolio and prepare a guidance note.** Develop guidelines for assessing project emissions and reporting portfolio emissions in line with the Technical Working Group of the International Financial Institutions and release them with a guidance note.	31 Dec 2024	CCSD, SPD, ORM
H.2.	**Strengthen instruments tracking ADB's exposure.**		
	1. **Enhance analytics of climate financial risk and management policy frameworks.** Develop, review, and implement methodologies and policies to manage climate financial risks. Develop and promote climate and disaster risk analytic tools to build capacity for risk-based decision making and management of financial exposure. Support the application of frameworks to assess existing modalities and instruments that address climate risk factors, including macro approaches such as fiscal and regulatory policies, compensation schemes offering subsidies and incentives, and forms of risk transfer. Support the application of frameworks to integrate climate science into underwriting practices to enhance the commercial viability of investment in low-carbon projects and to design and structure financial vehicles and instruments, such as blended finance coupled with concessional finance through guarantees and first-loss positions.	30 Jun 2026 (frameworks to be established)	ORM

continued on next page

Table continued

Action		Target Date	Responsibility
H.3.	**Provide adequate workforce to deliver the Climate Change Action Plan.**		
	1. **Assess workforce requirements to deliver the climate ambition and provide adequate staff resources.** Use the workforce rebalancing framework and internal administrative expenses.	31 Dec 2024	BPMSD
	2. **Establish a climate change staff development initiative, complete two cohorts of a climate leadership program, and pilot sector staff programs for seven sector and thematic groups in partnership with the sector groups.** Establish capacity development initiatives to ensure that sector and thematic groups have the climate and sector expertise to systematically integrate climate into all ADB investments. Complete the customized training program for senior management to steer ADB's climate shift.	30 Jun 2025	BPMSD

ADB = Asian Development Bank, ADF 13 or 14 = 13th or 14th replenishment of the Asian Development Fund, BPMSD = Budget, Personnel, and Management Systems Department, CAREC = Central Asia Regional Economic Cooperation, CCSD = Climate Change and Sustainable Development Department, CSD = Corporate Services Department, CSO = civil society organization, CTL = Controller's Department, CWRD = Central and West Asia Department, DMC = developing member country, DOCK = Department of Communications and Knowledge Management, ERDI = Economic Research and Development Impact Department, GHG = greenhouse gas, ITD = Information Technology Department; OMDP = Office of Markets Development and Public–Private Partnership, ORM = Office of Risk Management, PARD = Pacific Department, PPFD = Procurement, Portfolio, and Financial Management Department, PSOD = Private Sector Operations Department, RD = regional department, SARD = South Asia Department, SG = Sectors Group, SG-AFNR = Agriculture, Food, Nature, and Rural Development Sector Office, SG-ENE = Energy Sector Office, SG-FIN = Finance Office Group, SG-HSD = Human and Social Development Sector Office, SG-PSMG = Public Sector Management and Governance Sector Office, SG-TRA = Transport Sector Office, SG-WUD = Water and Urban Development Sector Office, SPD = Strategy, Policy, and Partnerships Department, TA = technical assistance.

[a] More sector-specific actions in Appendix 2.

Source: Asian Development Bank.

Appendix 2: Climate action by sector

1   AGRICULTURE, FOOD, NATURE, AND RURAL DEVELOPMENT

Opportunities for low-carbon and climate-resilient development

Agrifood systems contribute almost a third of global greenhouse gas (GHG) emissions. Livestock and rice are major emitters of methane. Agrochemical production, agrifood processing, and supply chain logistics are highly energy intensive. Most Asian Development Bank (ADB) climate investments in the sector so far have focused on adaptation, not yet fully exploiting nature-based opportunities for critical carbon reduction and removal. Leveraging green and blue finance and cofinancing, ADB can generate substantial new cash flow into rural communities and the private sector to incentivize the adoption of mitigation and adaptation activities at scale.

While well over $200 billion is needed every year to achieve the climate transition in the agrifood system, only $28.5 billion in climate finance was mobilized for the sector in 2019–2020, which is only 4.3% of the total global climate finance tracked at the project level.[46] There is a global imperative to multiply these investments by at least sevenfold.

The agrifood system in Asia is dominated by 400 million smallholder farmers, who are among the people most affected by climate change. Training farmers in climate-smart agriculture is critical for a just transition to net zero, as is supporting the decarbonization of agrifood companies.

GHG emitters and sinks. Livestock and rice generate substantial GHG emissions but are also significant sources of farmer livelihood. ADB will help reduce emission intensity and promote carbon sequestration activities that benefit farmers, such as regenerative agriculture and agroforestry.

Conventional fertilizers are a major source of emissions. Governments could repurpose fertilizer subsidies to promote greener alternatives. Innovation from the private sector should be promoted for all agricultural inputs, providing seed and preferring biological fertilizer and protection from pests and disease.

Smallholder farmers can help preserve and restore natural capital assets, many of which are major carbon sinks. It is essential to support government and private sector policies that avoid deforestation. Smallholder farmers need support, however, to make these policies a reality. ADB will increase investment in nature-based climate solutions, including landscape approaches, biodiversity conservation, sustainable forest management, agroforestry, and mangrove conservation.

Agrifood systems depend heavily on fossil fuels, particularly for processing and transportation. Renewable energy and energy efficiency should be promoted. Reducing food losses would shrink the sector's carbon footprint. Multisector projects and the promotion of public–private agrifood value chains provide opportunities to shrink carbon footprints and strengthen resilience across entire value chains.

---

[46]   City Policy Initiative. 2023. Landscape of Climate Finance for Agrifood Systems.

Water problems. Climate-resilient food production systems require reliable irrigation, achieved by modernizing irrigation infrastructure and strengthening management and information systems to minimize water and food production losses. Adverse impacts from climate change—droughts, floods, sea-level rise, and violent storms—are substantially water problems. Therefore, investment in climate-smart water management is essential, both on the farm and across the watershed.

Systems that disseminate climate information using cost-effective digital agricultural services can be critical adaptation investments incorporated into agriculture, food, and natural resource projects. Policy reform should repurpose agricultural subsidies and incentivize climate-smart agriculture. Alignment with Article 6 of the Paris Agreement is also important in leveraging private sector finance for upscaling climate investment in the sector.

Barriers to low-carbon and climate-resilient development

Traditional farming often uses resource-intensive processes such as land clearance, excessive water use, and agrochemical application. These practices worsen GHG emissions and otherwise diminish sector capacity to mitigate climate change. Transitioning to sustainable agricultural techniques demands a fundamental shift in farmer practice and mindset. Challenges to this shift arise from financial constraints, deeply ingrained cultural practices, and farmers having little access to modern knowledge and training. Smallholder farmers are highly risk-averse because their entire livelihood depends on their next harvest. Even simple changes of practice require a significant leap of faith, which can be made easier for farmers by training and demonstration farms, access to high-quality agricultural inputs and equipment, targeted subsidies, payment for ecosystem services, affordable financing, crop insurance, and guaranteed offtake.

Vulnerability to weather and high costs up front depressing investment. The unpredictability of weather poses another significant barrier. As extreme weather events such as droughts, floods, and heatwaves become more frequent and severe, they disrupt agriculture, reducing crop yields, causing livestock losses, and making smallholder farmers more vulnerable. This discourages long-term planning and investment in climate-resilient agricultural strategies. A lack of well-managed water storage and irrigation systems is a related barrier to climate resilience. Farmers require modern irrigation systems that provide assured but flexible water supply.

Inadequate technological adoption and innovation hinder climate action in the sector. While high-quality agricultural inputs and equipment, precision agriculture, hydroponics, and agroforestry offer promising avenues for reducing emissions and increasing productivity, their adoption is uneven and generally low. High costs up front, a lack of access to information, and resistance to change can prevent the integration of these technological innovations into traditional agricultural systems.

Market and policy obstacles. Poor market access and value chain complexities exacerbate other barriers. It is often difficult for smallholder farmers to access global markets and value supply chains to get fair prices. These barriers restrict their capacity to invest in climate-friendly practices and technologies. Additionally, inadequate postharvest storage and transportation systems cause food waste and thus amplify the carbon footprint of the sector.

Policy and regulatory obstacles loom large as hindrances to climate action. Policies are often fragmented locally and incoherent across a landscape, impeding the adoption of comprehensive strategies to ensure food security and reduce emissions. Subsidies can be disincentives for change by encouraging unsustainably excessive use of fertilizer and fossil fuels, especially in the absence of incentives to adopt sustainable methods. A harmonized policy framework that aligns economic incentives with environmental goals is essential to drive climate-friendly transformation in agriculture.

Good practices for low-carbon and climate-resilient development

ADB private sector investments already support good practices that can be replicated by other investors and promoted through sovereign or private sector financing channels. Examples include climate-smart fertilizers (Smartchem in India), climate-resilient animal feed (Abis in India and De Heus in Cambodia), climate-controlled greenhouse horticulture (Hasfarm in Viet Nam and in the People's Republic of China [PRC]), less carbon-intense livestock production (New Hope and Tianzow in the PRC), sustainable and climate-resilient aquaculture (Australis in Viet Nam), agroforestry systems (Olam, ECOM, LDC, and DSNG in Indonesia, Papua New Guinea, Timor-Leste, and Viet Nam), and energy-efficient food logistics and green buildings in food retail (Dali in the Philippines).

With support from the Pilot Program for Climate Resilience of Climate Investment Funds, ADB helped the Government of Cambodia prepare the Strategic Program for Climate Resilience, consisting of seven investment projects and, to provide overarching support for them, one technical assistance project. The Climate Resilient Rice Commercialization Sector Development Project is one of two investment projects in agriculture. It aims to help farmers increase rice production in the three largest rice-producing provinces—Battambang, Kampong Thom, and Prey Veng—by rehabilitating and climate-proofing irrigation systems and other rural infrastructure. Engineering was integrated into infrastructure design to cope with rapid flows of flood water. To reduce climate risks to rice production, the project is pilot testing in selected areas a weather-indexed crop insurance scheme. It is improving the availability and quality of rice seed by developing a certification system that will enable a more resilient crop. Finally, the project creates jobs for women. In sum, it strengthens the economic, social, and environmental sustainability of rice farming in Cambodia.

In India, integrated water resource management and water governance were improved with the establishment and operationalization of the Advanced Centre for Integrated Water Resources Management for preparing the state water policy and comprehensive river basin management plans under the Karnataka Integrated and Sustainable Water Resources Management Investment Program. Modernization is critical to improve aging and outdated irrigation systems across Karnataka. More efficient water use has allowed water to be reallocated to other areas for irrigation and other uses. Similarly, support for irrigation modernization has been provided across Indonesia.

Table A2.1: Actions for low-carbon and climate-resilient agricultural development

Action	Target Date
Considerably enhance collaboration between sovereign and nonsovereign operations. Cross-fertilize good practice in climate finance across ADB financing channels: sovereign, direct nonsovereign, and nonsovereign through financial intermediaries.	Ongoing
Strengthen collaboration with partners in agriculture, food, and natural resources (AFNR). Collaborate with the International Rice Research Institute to scale up the dissemination of low-carbon rice practice regionally and in individual countries through scoping analysis, business partnerships to support the bundle of required interventions, and the development of carbon credit projects with groups of smallholder farmers in South and Southeast Asia. Collaborate with the International Food Policy Research Institute (IFPRI) HarvestPlus program to scale up climate- and nutrition-smart solutions and address micronutrient deficiency in ADB project areas through seed multiplication and, to disseminate zinc- and iron-biofortified grain in India and Pakistan, value chain development working with women's groups. Enhance collaboration with the private sector on decarbonization and resilience.	Ongoing
Improve access to finance and knowledge. Forge partnerships with donors like the Global Environment Facility, Green Climate Fund, and Global Agriculture and Food Security Program—and with philanthropic foundations such as the Bill & Melinda Gates Foundation, Bloomberg, and the Bezos Earth Fund—to improve access to financing. Develop knowledge partnerships with IFPRI, CGIAR, Stanford University, Harvard University, and the private sector to access a pool of world's leading experts in climate-smart agriculture and nature-based solutions to design evidence-based projects for climate action in agriculture. Nurture partnerships with bilateral donors such as Australia and Canada to direct more blended finance to private sector investments in AFNR.	Ongoing
Improve integrated water resource management. Help developing member countries strengthen their policies and institutions for integrated water resource management and modernize their aging irrigation systems.	Ongoing
Announce ADB's natural capital ambition. Launch an innovative program to support net zero and a just transition in agrifood systems, which can include commitment from developing member countries to repurpose retrograde public subsidies.	31 Dec 2024
Adopt product-agnostic approaches to identifying high-impact climate interventions. Undertake sector diagnostics on AFNR development with a view to identifying potential investments, sovereign and nonsovereign, to foster greater collaboration across sovereign teams and the Private Sector Operations Department.	Ongoing
Make 90% of incremental investments in AFNR climate-smart. Apply a climate lens to all investments in the sector to enable emission reduction and adaptation and boost productivity.	31 Dec 2025

Source: Asian Development Bank.

2 ENERGY

Opportunities for low-carbon and climate-resilient development

ADB will help developing member countries (DMCs) improve energy efficiency, transition to renewable and low-carbon energy, and integrate climate and disaster resilience into energy sector operations. It will no longer finance new coal-fired power and heating plants but instead help DMCs phase out coal across Asia and the Pacific, as planned, and foster a just transition that considers impacts on people and communities. ADB support for clean and sustainable energy solutions—such as energy efficiency in both supply and demand, renewable energy, distributed renewable energy generation, and electric mobility—will make cities more livable by improving ambient air quality, as called for by Operational Priorities 3 and 4 of Strategy 2030. ADB will support associated infrastructure such as smart and resilient power grids and battery energy storage systems to ensure integration as the share of energy from renewable sources rises. When investing in energy infrastructure, ADB respects environmental safeguards to maintain biodiversity and healthy ecosystems.

Climate mitigation. ADB will facilitate the transition to sustainable, lower-carbon, and resilient energy systems by helping DMCs (i) accelerate their deployment of renewable energy, (ii) pursue strategic decarbonization and phase out coal, (iii) strengthen the climate resilience of energy infrastructure and ensure a just transition, and (iv) end environmental degradation from energy projects by prioritizing ecologically friendly technology.

Disaster resilience. Resilience is the ability to withstand extreme events and recover quickly. For infrastructure, resilience pertains not only to robust and durable physical assets. It describes the ability of infrastructure to buffer society from shocks and crises. Resilience derives from inclusive infrastructure that helps the most vulnerable segments of society withstand shocks. To enhance disaster resilience in the energy sector, advanced economies in the region have made grids highly redundant or shifted vulnerable overhead lines underground. Such measures are costly and perhaps unaffordable to DMCs whose priorities are to extend service to unserved areas or strengthen the grid to tackle serious service deficits. However, not investing in resilience can incur higher lifecycle costs because of infrastructure failure and repairs after extreme events.

Barriers to low-carbon and climate-resilient development

Coal and other fossil fuels have played a major role in providing energy in Asia and the Pacific and enabling regional economic development. Continued fossil fuel use, however, harms the environment and hastens climate change. In 2019, half of global carbon dioxide (CO_2) emissions from coal, oil, and natural gas came from Asia and the Pacific. Fossil fuels are similarly the main source of local air pollutants that cause immediate and lasting harm to public health and ecosystems. Some of the most polluted cities in the world in terms of annual average particulate concentration are in Asia and the Pacific. Consequently, the energy sector in Asia and the Pacific is a critical area for direct and effective response to climate change, and for building climate and disaster resilience. Deep and long engagement in the sector uniquely positions ADB to play a pivotal role.

Energy challenges and emerging needs. DMCs need to ensure (i) universal household access to electricity and clean cooking, heating, and cooling options; (ii) energy security to support economic growth; (iii) financial viability, effective and sustainable operation and maintenance, resilience under climate change and extreme events, climate change mitigation through lower carbon use, and more benign health and environmental impacts; and (iv) good sector regulations and governance, utility performance, and private sector participation. While many DMCs have made significant progress in these areas, they need continued support to consolidate achievements and address emerging challenges and opportunities.

Today, DMCs are challenged to accommodate a large role for renewable energy, sustainably distribute energy resources, and garner demand-side participation in power system operation. Governments continue to deregulate and reform their power sectors to increase efficiency and restructure state-owned utilities to allow competition. New power exchanges will likely emerge, and existing ones be strengthened. Newer power generation technology and fuels are overtaking fossil fuels in terms of pricing that considers social and environmental costs through carbon taxes, emission trading systems, and international offset mechanisms. However, issues persist in many countries in the region regarding cost-reflective tariffs and governance measures to ensure sector accountability and sustainability. Greater flexibility to accommodate new technologies will require reform to governance, markets, and DMC regulations.

Old subsidies and new. Subsidies have long been used to promote desired energy objectives. They have made energy affordable, with automotive fuels in particular subsidized to ensure economic productivity and mobility and to improve the quality of life. More recently, subsidies have accelerated the deployment of renewable energy. Fossil fuel subsidies are typically concentrated in upstream wholesale energy production and distribution operations such as coal mining and petroleum fuel supply, while renewable energy subsidies are typically concentrated at the project and retail end of the supply chain, such as rooftop solar panels. Such financial incentives as feed-in tariffs for renewable energy are now being eliminated or reduced as renewable energy becomes more competitive.

To avoid unwanted market distortion and promote economic efficiency, energy subsidies should be targeted, timebound, and transparent across the full spectrum of fuel types and energy services. Targeting subsidies to achieve their objectives without unintended consequences remains an important policy challenge in the region.

Investment in energy security after the pandemic. As the region recovers from coronavirus disease (COVID-19), improving resilience and security in the energy sector is clearly identified as a priority. Institutional capacity building remains key to achieving good governance. While energy systems have generally operated well so far, their typical reliance on imported expertise, technology, and fossil fuels leaves them vulnerable. When manufactured, deployed, and maintained locally, renewable energy has potential to be a resilient, indigenous resource. COVID-19 temporarily reduced the cost of imported fossil fuels by hitting demand, but the recent crisis exposed DMCs to risks regarding access to fossil fuels and price volatility.

Reduced use of imported fuel therefore augments resilience in DMC energy systems. Meanwhile, the increased use of information and communication technology in energy infrastructure requires a new focus on cybersecurity to avoid security threats. Given their need to invest a combined $800 billion per year in energy, ADB DMCs are well advised to pursue reform that creates more opportunity for private sector participation, particularly in electricity generation. While fully open and competitive electricity markets are still rare in the region, many DMCs have enabled private investment through regulated entry points such as public–private partnerships, renewable energy auctions, and independent power producers with long-term power purchase agreements. ADB will continue to mobilize more concessional financing, technical support, and catalytic activity for private sector investment, innovation, and affordable transfer of green technology.

Good practices for low-carbon and climate-resilient development

ADB incorporates the social cost of carbon across all operations, including in energy. The unit value used by ADB, $46.10/ton of CO_2 equivalent in 2021, is based on Intergovernmental Panel on Climate Change empirical estimates of the global social cost of carbon as reported in its Fifth Assessment Report. This is increased by 2% annually in real terms to allow for potential increase in marginal damage from global warming. This unit value is used in economic analyses to estimate the damage created by projects that increase emissions and the value of avoided GHG emissions for projects that reduce emissions. The unit value will be revised in the future with the availability of more and newer estimates of damage caused by climate change.

Examples of projects:

(i) India: Demand-Side Energy Efficiency Sector Project
(ii) Kyrgyz Republic: Uch-Kurgan Hydropower Plant Modernization Project
(iii) PRC: Air Quality Improvement in the Greater Beijing–Tianjin–Hebei Region
(iv) Azerbaijan: Alat Solar Power Project
(v) Uzbekistan: Solar Public–Private Partnership Investment Program

Examples of energy transition projects:

(i) **South Tarawa Renewable Energy Project**. Approved in December 2020, this first ADB energy project in Kiribati is to install a climate-resilient ground-mounted solar photovoltaic and battery energy storage system with rainwater harvesting and an enhanced tree-planting program. The project is funded by $8.0 million from ADB, $2.0 million from the New Zealand Ministry of Foreign Affairs and Trade, and $3.7 million from the Strategic Climate Fund.
(ii) **Sri Lanka Wind Power Generation Project**. This was approved in October 2017 to enhance access to clean, renewable, and reliable power supply. The project increased wind power generation by (a) constructing a 100 megawatt (MW) wind park—the first of this size in Sri Lanka—on Mannar Island in Northern Province; (b) developing wind park infrastructure; and (c) establishing a renewable energy dispatch control center to forecast, control, and manage intermittent 100 MW wind power generation. Construction is completed, and the wind park is operational. Innovative technology minimizes impact on bird and bat flight paths.
(iii) **Southern Thailand Wind Power and Battery Energy Storage Project**. Approved in January 2020, the project is the first private sector project in Thailand to integrate utility-scale wind power generation with battery energy storage. It will have an important demonstration effect.

Table A2.2: Actions for low-carbon and climate-resilient energy development

Action	Target Date
Harness synergies between sector investments. Emphasize infrastructure that delivers energy, mobility, and the transport of goods; access to water, sanitation, and waste management; and manufacturing and light-industry activities that provide jobs, while protecting and where possible enhancing public spaces and health.	Ongoing
Scale up investment and mobilize new types of transformation-enabling infrastructure. Develop and finance electric vehicle charging facilities, green hydrogen, renewable energy from battery-hybrid systems, infrastructure that promotes circular economy approaches, flood defense, low-carbon water production facilities, and digital infrastructure including early warning and early action systems, and social protection for disaster readiness.	Ongoing
Identify deep decarbonizing opportunities in key industries. Starting with technical assistance and building on early-stage work done in Southeast Asia, invest significant staff time and effort in identifying deep decarbonization opportunities in cement, steel, other manufacturing, and construction, and in public and private building management.	Ongoing Starting in January 2024
Scale up investment and mobilize to replace and retrofit large single-source emitters and climate-vulnerable infrastructure. Develop and finance energy-efficiency and fuel-switching solutions in manufacturing; leverage green-equipment facilities to support the import, trade, and production of low-carbon technologies; and upgrade or rehabilitate vulnerable infrastructure such as road and rail networks, power transmission and distribution systems, and water supply infrastructure.	Ongoing
Support the development of climate-smart infrastructure design standards. Support in addition green building standards and the regional adoption of energy-efficient design standards for key technologies.	Ongoing
Adopt product-agnostic approaches to identifying high-impact climate interventions in energy and related industrial sectors. Require all sector teams to undertake sector diagnostics with a view to identifying potential investments, sovereign and nonsovereign, to foster greater collaboration across sovereign teams and the Private Sector Operations Department.	Ongoing

Source: Asian Development Bank.

3 FINANCE

Opportunities for low-carbon and climate-resilient development

Finance is critical to accelerating climate mitigation and adaptation; mainstreaming the transition to a net-zero economy; strengthening disaster resilience; and supporting micro, small, and medium-sized enterprises (MSMEs), in particular those owned and operated by women. These opportunities are expected to grow with policy reform, capacity building, and DMC pipeline development. Enhanced climate resilience and low-carbon development requires economies to transition from current high-emitting industries and technologies. The finance sector needs to go beyond green finance to bridge the financing gap and support a transition to net-zero pathways.

Reform to scale up climate finance. Central to the ability to deliver climate finance is regulatory and policy reform, notably to advance strategies to attract private financing and enable policies, regulations, and frameworks for (i) green, blue, and other thematic bonds; (ii) improved disclosure and reporting; and (iii) strengthened verification processes. A developed capital market is critical to efficiently mobilizing climate finance. Proportionate and balanced regulation of capital markets is needed to strengthen regulatory regimes for pension funds, insurance companies, and investment schemes.

Growing demand for finance. As climate adaptation and mitigation regulations and policy are enhanced, and as financial institutions build their internal capacity, strong demand is expected for climate finance products and funds to manage physical and transition risks from climate change.

Large blended finance operations and technical assistance programs and grants are needed to help clients in DMCs prepare bankable and sustainable projects and programs. Thematic bonds for sustainable projects and long-term and blended funding—such as through financial intermediation loans for climate mitigation, adaptation, and transition—will narrow the financing gap for climate projects and address the regional infrastructure deficit. Islamic finance has potential in Muslim DMCs as an avenue for expansion.

Nature-based solutions will be harnessed to safeguard ecosystems, restore land and water resources, promote sustainable agriculture, enhance marine and ocean health, and preserve biodiversity. They may be supported through domestic capital markets and other financial products.

Acute climate impacts on DMCs create a pressing need for disaster risk finance. ADB will design financial risk protection for crop and livestock losses, MSMEs, and losses along the value chain from disasters. Microinsurance offers opportunities.

Digital finance and innovative solutions. These options have rapidly increased in sovereign and nonsovereign operations alike to enhance climate resilience and mitigation. Critical areas for ADB support are technology to enhance and support environmental, social, and governance initiatives, such as platforms for digital bond issuance and investment, climate fintech, carbon-trading platforms, and digital tools for measuring green and climate finance data.

Underserved segments of the population, including women, are a key area for the finance sector to accelerate, ensuring that climate finance reaches these clients. Digital finance can significantly enhance MSME competitiveness, resilience, and growth.

Barriers to low-carbon and climate-resilient development

Some DMCs address environmental and climate issues by developing long-term strategies and policy frameworks: national and local green growth strategies, low-emission economic development strategies, renewable energy targets, and Paris Agreement nationally determined contributions (NDCs). However, many DMCs still lack coherent policy frameworks and need additional financial resources for climate mitigation and adaptation.

Implementing the right policy mix will be vital for the transition to a low-carbon, climate-resilient future that can address climate change and sustain recovery from COVID-19. The successful implementation of green and climate finance in the region must overcome four barriers:

(i) **Constrained fiscal space.** Challenges to mitigating climate change are daunting. The need for climate adaptation has never been more urgent, but the pandemic constrained in many DMCs the fiscal space needed to undertake the actions required to recover from COVID-19 and address climate change.

(ii) **Weak institutional capacity and underdeveloped capital markets.** Despite the important role of financial institutions in enhancing climate action, many constraints hinder the ability of finance institutions to channel private sector finance. Institutional weakness and a lack of internal capacity and incentives are major causes of lagging climate response in Asia and the Pacific. Additionally, finance institutions lack long-term access to funds available at a competitive price, which is needed to facilitate many climate projects. Moreover, domestic capital markets are underdeveloped in many DMCs and cannot effectively attract and channel private sector funding to these projects.

(iii) **Policy and regulatory gaps.** Scaling up green and climate finance entails transforming business and investment policies beyond those directly applicable to green and climate finance. Among the multiple factors that can block green and climate finance are the broader legal system and policy environment, which influence investment decisions. If the legal and regulatory system is unclear or contradictory, it can create unintended barriers, leaving a country less likely to attract necessary climate finance.

(iv) **Lack of investment-ready projects.** A significant barrier to climate finance in the region is a lack of projects identifiable as investment ready. Despite increased demand for green projects, many DMCs in the region do not meet accepted risk-management criteria for investment, depriving vulnerable countries of investment flows.

Good practices for low-carbon and climate-resilient development

ADB can help DMCs achieve climate change impacts beyond what ADB direct climate investment alone can support.

Aligning investment and its lending portfolio with the Paris Agreement, ADB will offer policy-based and financial-intermediation loans to help DMCs meet their ambitious climate mitigation and adaptation goals. While policy-based loans are used to set frameworks and achieve essential reform, financial intermediation loans address market failures in climate change mitigation and a clean-energy transition. ADB will work across existing modalities and instruments that either reduce risk by improving the policy and regulatory environment, transfer risk to other participants, or compensate for risk through direct financial incentives. ADB will continue to build domestic capital markets to crowd in private sector funding.

ADB will examine the role of public policy in making available domestic private finance for low-carbon investment. It will identify emerging asset classes, sources of domestic financing, and capital market solutions for low-carbon infrastructure, such as green bonds and impact investment, as sources of low-cost, high-impact, and longer-term financing. ADB will apply financial expertise and climate science to pricing models and integrate climate risks into underwriting practices and investment analysis. Mandating catastrophe insurance for critical infrastructure will enhance resilience. In addition, more active participation by private sector funds can be enabled by helping DMCs develop and use diverse and innovative green financial approaches and instruments: green investment banks, green bonds, social bonds, sustainability-linked bonds, thematic bonds including asset-backed security, and climate credit mechanisms.

A just transition. ADB will assess approaches, policies, instruments, and activities—including incentives such as de-risking measures related to transition finance—to help DMCs transition to a net-zero economy. Developing and expanding transition finance instruments such as debt, bond, and risk-mitigation financial products will be pursued to enable the climate transition. ADB will support a just transition as businesses start moving to net zero by evaluating the risk of stranded assets and expanding the role of transition finance to help high-carbon industries implement long-term changes to become greener. It will help financial institutions strengthen climate-related risk management and manufacturing MSMEs adopt green technology. Importantly, ADB will catalyze private sector funding for low-carbon technology in the energy and transport sectors.

Examples of financial intermediation loans:

(i) India: Accelerating Environmental, Social Infrastructure Investment Facility (approval expected in 2024)
(ii) Indonesia: Sustainable Development Goals Indonesia One—Green Finance Facility (Phase One)
(iii) Mongolia: Supporting the Credit Guarantee System for Economic Diversification and Employment Project
(iv) PRC: Shandong Green Development Fund Project
(v) PRC: Bank of Qingdao Blue Finance Project
(vi) PRC: Bank of Xingtai Green Finance Development Project
(vii) PRC: Bank of Huzhou Decarbonizing Micro, Small, and Medium-Sized Enterprises Project
(viii) PRC: Promoting Industrial Park Green and Low-Carbon Transition Project (under processing)
(ix) PRC: Hainan Disaster Risk Finance and Resilience Innovation Project (under processing)
(x) PRC: Guangxi Environmentally Sustainable Rural Development Demonstration (under processing)
(xi) Samoa: Agribusiness Support Project
(xii) Sri Lanka: Enhancing Small and Medium-sized Enterprises Project (formerly Small and Medium-sized Enterprises Credit Guarantee Institution Project)

Other examples:

(i) Bangladesh: Strengthening the Capacity of Infrastructure Development Company Limited
(ii) Bhutan: Financial Market Development Program
(iii) India: Green Climate Finance Facility (expected approval in 2024)
(iv) Kazakhstan: Supporting Development of Innovative Green Housing Finance
(v) Mongolia: Climate Change Support Program (policy-based loan under processing)
(vi) Philippines: Support to Capital Market Generated Infrastructure Financing Program (Subprogram 2)
(vii) Sri Lanka: Financial Sector Stability and Reforms Program (Subprogram 1)

Examples of green and sustainable finance projects:

(i) **Sustainable Development Goals Indonesia One—Green Finance Facility.** This $150 million financial intermediary loan to Indonesia supports Sustainable Development Goal achievement. Its innovative transition financing mechanism links fund provision to subprojects with clear green and financial bankability targets. Designed as a de-risking facility, the project aims to leverage ADB and government funds to catalyze multiple green funds from private, institutional, and commercial sources.
(ii) **Climate Change Support Program for Mongolia.** This $100 million loan proposal, expected to be approved in 2024, will promote, as its core objective, complementary medium-term structural reform to support critical climate change actions. The policy-based loan will leverage critical policy reform and redirect planning and finance to accelerate investment in climate adaptation and mitigation.
(iii) **Hainan Disaster Risk Finance and Resilience Innovation Project.** This $150 million financial intermediation loan proposal, expected to be approved in 2024, supports a comprehensive disaster risk financing mechanism, as well as a provincial public finance framework and a disaster risk funding pool.

(iv) **Enhancing Small and Medium-sized Enterprises Finance Project in Sri Lanka**. This $100 million financial intermediation loan proposal, expected to be approved in 2023, will make adaptation and mitigation finance more available to small and medium-sized enterprises through a dedicated line of credit and the establishment of a national institution offering credit guarantees. This will support the country's NDC and facilitate underlying loans that finance climate adaptation and mitigation.

(v) **Accelerating Environmental Social Infrastructure Investment Facility.** This $500 million financial intermediation loan proposal, expected to be approved in 2024, will enable India Infrastructure Finance Company Limited to provide long-term funds to infrastructure projects pursued as public–private partnerships. The project supports climate change through a two-pronged approach: (a) mobilizing funds for green energy generation that leverage private sector financing, and (b) improving climate risk management.

(vi) **Green Bond Investment in Mongolia.** A $20 million green bond investment to be listed on the Mongolian Stock Exchange to fund green investments qualified under the Mongolian Green Taxonomy and Khan Bank's Green Investment Framework. This is processed by the Private Sector Operations Department (PSOD), Finance Office Group (SG-FIN), and East Asia Department (EARD). Proposed TA for promoting innovative and sustainable financing, processed by SG-FIN, will support banks, including Khan Bank as a pilot, to strengthen capacity on green and sustainable finance.

(vii) **Financing Micro, Small, and Medium-Sized Enterprises and Promoting Green Lending Activities in Mongolia.** The project will be jointly processed by PSOD, SG-FIN, and EARD. Proposed TA processed by SG-Fin will strengthen capacity in banks, including Bogd Bank as a pilot, on green and sustainable finance.

Table A2.3: Actions for low-carbon and climate-resilient finance development

Action	Target Date
Develop voluntary guidance for financial institutions on phasing out coal-fired power plants in Asia. Working with the Glasgow Financial Alliance for Net Zero, Asia Pacific Network, focus the guidance note on financial viability through the use of financial levers appropriate to Asia and the Pacific.	30 Nov 2023
Prepare frameworks for disaster and pandemic risk financing and feasibility studies on disaster insurance products. Publish country assessments for Cambodia, the Kyrgyz Republic, Pakistan, and the Philippines on the enabling environment for disaster and pandemic risk financing and identify actions to advance the availability and uptake of risk financing. Develop feasibility studies to inform the design of insurance pilots for post-disaster livelihood and small business restoration in Nepal.	30 June 2024
Support regional cooperation initiatives on climate and transition finance. Foster regional cooperation with finance sector teams collaborating closely with regional cooperation initiative teams in regional departments to build on successful support to the ASEAN Capital Markets Forum of the Association of Southeast Asian Nations, the Southeast Asia Development Symposium, and the Southeast Asia Green Finance Hub. Perhaps include initiatives to develop green taxonomies and share knowledge on green bond issuance programs.	Ongoing
Deliver country assessments and policy recommendations. Assess micro- and macroprudential regulations, market conduct, and governance frameworks for banks, insurance companies, and capital markets in Bangladesh, Indonesia, Mongolia, the Philippines, and Viet Nam to enhance climate and disaster resilience in financial systems by catalyzing climate finance to promote climate adaptation and mitigation. To make low-carbon and climate-resilient investments more attractive, assessments will identify barriers that impede efforts by developing member countries to decarbonize, enhance understanding of climate finance deployment, and recommend policy measures to address the barriers.	31 Mar 2026
Adopt product-agnostic approaches to identify high-impact climate interventions in the finance sector. Require all sector teams to undertake sector diagnostics with a view to identifying potential investments, sovereign and nonsovereign, to foster greater collaboration across sovereign teams and the Private Sector Operations Department.	Ongoing

Source: Asian Development Bank.

4 HUMAN AND SOCIAL DEVELOPMENT

Opportunities for low-carbon and climate-resilient development

Leadership on climate and health is pivotal for the well-being of the world's 8 billion people, particularly those in low- and middle-income countries. Only four countries in the world emit more climate pollution than the global health-care industry, which has potential to triple its emissions by 2050. It is critical for the health sector to reach net-zero emissions in line with the Paris Agreement while maintaining core health system functions to protect populations from climate change, for example vaccinating vulnerable communities for flood-induced infectious diseases or treating severe malnutrition from drought. Health systems themselves remain vulnerable to climate change, as facilities are often not climate-proofed, and the workforce has not been trained on emerging climate diseases and disasters. Despite the dire health implications of climate change and the urgent need for synergistic solutions, little awareness of the climate–health nexus exists, and few initiatives are funded.

Education systems with strong emergency response capacity will be critical to minimize damage and disruption from extreme climate events. Climate-smart education can equip learners with knowledge, skills, and values to adapt to climate change and act in sustainable societies. Higher education and technical and vocational education and training should, in partnership with the private sector, develop skills for jobs in the low-carbon and climate-resilient economy.

Climate-resilient social protection needs to be expanded, partly with innovative financial products such as social insurance schemes for climate catastrophes. Support for a just transition helps DMCs address social impacts as they shift their economies to low carbon to meet their NDCs.

Resilience in national development strategies. DMCs have started to include disaster and climate resilience in their national development strategies, which affect social sector strategies as they aim to build capacity and disaster and climate resilience. ADB will align investment with national adaptation plans and adopt a comprehensive climate-smart project design framework guided by these principles: (i) climate-proofing social service infrastructure, (ii) climate resilience in social services, and (iii) using social services to empower communities to become climate resilient and to scale up the application of climate finance to health, education, and social protection. ADB will strengthen results-based and policy-based lending in the social sectors and mainstream climate change interventions for mitigation and adaptation results.

Climate action through education. Five key opportunities make education a potent climate action platform:

(i) integrating sustainability across education by greening curricula, learning and assessment materials, teacher education, and competency standards;
(ii) building climate-resilient and sustainable education infrastructure for resilient and low-carbon learning environments;
(iii) promoting green workforce development for a just transition to clean energy, sustainable transport, low-carbon urban development, and nature-based solutions;
(iv) supporting research and development and business incubation for innovation and the adoption of climate technologies; and
(v) building capacity for community-led adaptation and climate resilience.

Principles to mainstream climate in the health agenda. ADB support to the Group of Twenty (G20) has been essential to mainstreaming climate in the health agenda. The G20 has endorsed key principles to guide health-related climate action to improve "health for all" and minimize the environmental impacts of health service delivery. These principles (i) prioritize climate-resilient health development, (ii) support the transition to sustainable and low-carbon health systems, (iii) decarbonize the health-care supply chain, (iv) mainstream resilient and sustainable health system resources, and (v) foster collaboration on interconnected human, animal, and climate health challenges. These principles embody a crosscutting One Health approach.

Barriers to low-carbon and climate-resilient development

There is not yet a strong body of knowledge on what works at the intersection of climate change and social development. Poverty, gender, and social analyses are needed to identify risks arising from climate change and the low-carbon transition. No national database to map and monitor climate-induced poverty has been established to inform the targeting of vulnerable populations. It is necessary to identify the poverty, gender, and other social dimensions of climate change impacts to optimize interventions. Existing social protection programs either do not cover climate shocks or are ineffective. Social protection often fails to reach intended beneficiaries or is insufficient to provide real protection. Climate-induced health problems and effective interventions have received little attention in DMCs.

Solutions that effectively mitigate climate risks to health, well-being, education, and human development encompass a broad spectrum of policies, strategies, and initiatives. For example, DMCs lack green building codes. Green schools and hospitals need to align with international codes that DMCs must endorse for each project. Cross-sector dialogue with DMCs on these endorsements will make civil works in the social sector more climate resilient and low carbon.

Deficient financing. Development financing is deficient for interventions at the intersection of climate change, health, and other social sectors. Further, DMCs allocate little capital or recurrent expenditure to social sectors to minimize energy consumption. Reducing energy consumption often requires investment in low-emission technologies, clean transportation, and climate-proofing facilities. While some low- and middle-income countries have developed national health adaptation plans, lack of funds and the COVID-19 pandemic have delayed their implementation. Investment should balance capital and recurrent expenditure in detail before a government raises budget allocations for social sectors.

Climate education is scarcely embedded in education strategies and delivery. The United Nations Educational, Scientific, and Cultural Organization (UNESCO) highlights that fewer than half of 100 reviewed countries had a climate change agenda in their national curriculum frameworks and scarcely refer to it in national determined contributions.[47] Among 58,000 teachers surveyed, 95% thought climate change education was important, but fewer than a quarter could describe appropriate climate action. Moreover, 70% of the youth surveyed know little or nothing about climate change.

Good practices for low-carbon and climate-resilient development

Thailand: Medical Excellence Centers Project. The proposed project envisages 30% climate financing to construct and equip medical excellence centers at five public hospitals. It has several climate elements: climate-smart infrastructure, assessments, and studies for climate change mitigation, as well as training on climate change adaptation and mitigation for health-care workers.

India: Early Childhood Development Project in Meghalaya Project. The project envisages about 40% ADB financing for climate adaptation, incorporating the institutionalization of climate resilience methods, clean and green technology for construction, and the operation of over 2,000 early childhood daycare centers across Meghalaya, a state in northwest India. It will train a frontline workforce for climate and disaster preparedness and improve response to climate risks challenging gender equity, social inclusion, and mental health. It will facilitate a transition from solid fuels like firewood and charcoal to cleaner fuels like natural gas for cooking in early child daycare facilities, complemented by a nutrition intervention through community-run kitchen gardens.

Pakistan: Integrated Social Protection Development Program. Climate-responsive social protection is supported by mapping the population vulnerable to climate-induced poverty, considering climate impact on poverty-targeting criteria, and strengthening the link with the National Socio-Economic Registry.

---

[47] UNESCO. 2022. Youth *Demands for Quality Climate Change Education*; and UNESCO. 2021. Skills *Development and Climate Action Plans*.

Table A2.4: Actions for low-carbon and climate-resilient human and social development

Action	Target Date
Develop and deliver green social sector infrastructure. (i) Invest in climate-resilient infrastructure and low-carbon school campuses and health facilities. (ii) Build capacity in social sector executing agencies, line ministries, facility management offices, and school administrations to plan, operate, and maintain disaster-resilient and energy-efficient social sector infrastructure. (iii) Develop a technical guidance note on climate-smart infrastructure design standards for social sector line ministries. (iv) Promote green accreditation for schools and higher education institutions.	31 Dec 2024
Develop and deliver climate education programs. (i) **Greening education.** Incorporate climate education into project designs across all levels of education, including the greening of teaching, learning, and assessment materials. (ii) **Cross-sectoral solutions.** Promote green workforce development and community climate resilience capacity building through cross-sectoral solutions in green investment, social protection, and climate adaptation projects. (iii) **Upstream diagnostics.** Conduct country-level green labor market and just transition assessments. (iv) **Green innovation.** Support higher education institutions in developing research and start-up incubation capacity for the development, promotion, and adoption of sustainable technologies. (v) **Knowledge work.** Conduct knowledge work and establish knowledge partnerships in fields related to climate education.	31 Dec 2025
Establish the Climate and Health Initiative to develop sustainable, climate-resilient, and low-carbon health systems and service delivery. Establish the Climate and Health Initiative as a partnership facility dedicated to consolidating, streamlining, and amplifying policy and practice at the intersection of climate change and health, and to serve other functions, notably knowledge generation, novel financing, forging partnerships, incubating innovation, building capacity, and advocacy. (i) Strengthen disease and climate-sensitive surveillance systems. (ii) Innovate crowdsourcing for, for example, solarized health facilities. (iii) De-carbonize health supply chains and medical waste systems and deliver sustainable vaccine manufacturing solutions. (iv) Support telemedicine for a smaller carbon footprint. (v) Support workforce capacity building on the climate and health nexus. (vi) Develop standardized country diagnostic and assessment tools and resources on climate and health. (vii) Strengthen policy frameworks and action plans for health and climate change. (viii) Strengthen disaster risk management systems.	Ongoing
Develop and implement social protection policies, programs, and systems for climate resilience and a just transition. (i) Strengthen poverty and social assessments to capture climate risks and vulnerabilities and thus inform social protection and other operations for climate adaptation and mitigation. (ii) Ensure that social protection registration and targeting efforts reflect the dynamic nature of poverty and vulnerability, particularly in the context of climate change. (iii) Identify opportunities to integrate climate risk and vulnerability data into national poverty analysis. (iv) Support partnerships and coordination across social protection, climate change, and disaster risk management actors to improve adaptive and shock-responsive social protection. (v) Develop a knowledge pillar for the just transition platform that includes evidence generation and dissemination for data-driven policy making. (vi) Invest in multisector cooperation to ensure a just transition through, for example, reskilling and upskilling efforts, green public works programs, social assistance linked with labor market interventions, unemployment benefits, decent work opportunities, and community development programs.	31 Dec 2025

continued on next page

Table continued

Action	Target Date
Green the midterm budget framework on social sectors. (i) Review government budget frameworks for social sectors to identify areas prime for greening reform, such as boosting capital expenditure on green buildings, renewable energy solutions for schools and hospitals, operating and maintenance expenses for climate-resilient facilities, and budget for climate-resilient social protection schemes. (ii) In sector-development, policy-based, and results-based operations, incorporate policies and strategic actions for government updates to the midterm budget framework in line with the dimensions enumerated above. (iii) Through blended financing mechanisms, pool public and private financing for health and climate change projects. This is particularly important as public sources are estimated to cover only about 10% of climate needs.	31 Dec 2025
Adopt product-agnostic approaches to identify high-impact climate interventions in human and social development. Require all sector teams to undertake sector diagnostics with a view to identifying potential investments, sovereign and nonsovereign, to foster greater collaboration across sovereign teams and the Private Sector Operations Department.	Ongoing

Source: Asian Development Bank.

5 PUBLIC SECTOR MANAGEMENT AND GOVERNANCE

Opportunities for low-carbon and climate-resilient development

The Public Sector Management and Governance Office (SG-PSMG) is a sector group with a critical role to play in enhancing climate-resilient and low-carbon development. By aligning with sector trends and priorities, adopting innovative strategies, and fostering collaboration, it can drive transformative change and ensure a sustainable and climate-resilient future in Asia and the Pacific.

Integrating climate into macro-fiscal frameworks. A key opportunity lies in embedding climate considerations into fiscal policies, regulations, and public financial management systems. Through policy dialogue and programmatic engagement, SG-PSMG will help DMCs design policies for pricing carbon emissions; design and adopt fiscal policies that promote clean technology; design climate-sensitive eco-fiscal transfer systems for DMCs with decentralized systems of governance; develop climate-smart fiscal rules; support the integration of climate and environmental considerations in public investment management practices; develop green taxonomies; define climate-related financial metrics, certification labels, and disclosure standards; develop climate-sensitive budget tracking systems; integrate climate risks into fiscal risk- and debt-management systems; incorporate climate considerations into central bank asset purchases; and develop legal and institutional frameworks for green procurement.

Leveraging public finance to mobilize private sector climate finances. To achieve this, SG-PSMG can provide support to DMCs to employ various strategies including (i) policy and regulations, (ii) public sector funding, (iii) collaboration with the private sector on sustainable infrastructure projects through PPP, (iv) selective and targeted tax incentives and credit enhancements, and (v) capacity development. By implementing these strategies, governments can create an environment that attracts private capital toward climate solutions, fostering a sustainable and resilient economy.

Strengthening climate governance and institutional capacity. Enhancing climate governance is critical for effective climate action. SG-PSMG will build capacity in public institutions to plan, implement, and monitor climate-resilient and low-carbon initiatives, perhaps by creating specialized units or task forces dedicated to climate issues and by injecting climate expertise into decision-making processes.

Climate challenges are multidimensional and require collaboration across sectors. SG-PSMG will facilitate collaboration among multiple sectors, government agencies, private sector entities, and civil society organizations. This approach will ensure integrated planning and coherent implementation of climate initiatives in transportation, energy, and urban planning.

Leveraging technology, innovation, and knowledge sharing. Embracing technology and innovation is crucial for low-carbon development. SG-PSMG will explore opportunities to leverage digital solutions, data analytics, and innovative financing mechanisms to drive climate initiatives. This may include using satellite imagery to assess disaster risk, or blockchain to transparently manage climate finance.

Access to accurate climate information is essential for informed decision-making. SG-PSMG will develop platforms for sharing climate data, research, and best practices to empower policy makers, practitioners, and the public with the information they need to design effective climate-resilient and low-carbon strategies.

Collaborative efforts are essential for comprehensive climate action. The sector can encourage partnerships between governments, private sector entities, academia, and civil society to jointly address challenges and develop innovative solutions.

Barriers to low-carbon and climate-resilient development

The pursuit of climate-resilient and low-carbon development in the public sector is a global imperative, yet it faces an array of barriers that hinder progress. Effectively addressing them requires comprehensive and collaborative efforts across various domains, ranging from policy formulation to public engagement.

Political economy challenges. A central challenge revolves around a lack of political will and leadership for considering climate in policy-making and decision-making processes. Resource allocation and action are then inadequate to bolster climate resilience and promote low-carbon initiatives. Further, the immediate need to meet short-term economic goals, often driven by electoral cycles, can overshadow longer-term climate objectives. Overcoming these challenges demands a sustainability ethos at the highest levels of government. Climate-resilient strategies require sustained investment and unwavering commitment achieved by ensuring that political agendas recognize the urgency of climate action.

Institutional, technical capacity, and financial constraints. Public sector institutional capacity is pivotal to success. However, many civil servants lack the technical expertise, knowledge, and resources needed to effectively plan and execute climate-resilient and low-carbon projects. Addressing this challenge requires enhanced institutional capability.

Budget limitations and competing priorities hinder investment in climate projects and other critical priorities, like infrastructure upgrades and technological transitions, that are crucial to reducing emissions and enhancing resilience. Access to climate finance is difficult, particularly for developing countries. Overcoming this barrier requires international cooperation, fiscal reform, and financial support to ensure that all DMCs can pursue climate resilience.

Unclear policy framework and public understanding. Incoherent public policy, often a result of conflicting objectives, can pull policy actions in opposing directions. For example, many countries tax fossil fuels, and some implement exemplary carbon tax systems, while at the same time offering direct and indirect subsidies for fossil fuel use, leaving net effective rates on carbon uncertain. Opposing policies are often administered by different government agencies working in isolation, making it impossible to resolve issues without political input. Further, while the private sector has a key role in low-carbon development, unclear regulations may dissuade private investment and collaboration in climate-friendly initiatives.

Low understanding of climate change undercuts demand for solutions, and insufficient public pressure on governments diminishes any sense of urgency. Further hampering the low-carbon transition is resistance to change for lack of awareness and reflecting vested interests and concern about job losses. Effective communication campaigns are vital to mobilize support.

Accurate and dependable climate data and risk assessments are essential to fill data and information gaps, formulate well-informed strategies, and monitor their implementation.

Good practices for low-carbon and climate-resilient development

Armenia: Fiscal Sustainability and Financial Markets Development Program. Subprogram 1, approved in 2022, promotes green and sustainable economic development by (i) securing government approval of a national plan for climate adaptation and the key principles to guide its integration into budget, policy, and programming, including the principle of climate-aligned financial decision-making and management; (ii) embedding disaster risk management and climate adaptation and mitigation objectives in key identification and prioritization criteria for investment projects; and (iii) formulating green economy policy and aligning green policy tools with the country's mitigation and adaptation actions. Subprogram 2 has follow-on action to deepen these reforms.

Uzbekistan: Economic Management Improvement Program. Subprogram 1, approved in 2023, takes a policy-based programmatic approach to help the Government of Uzbekistan strengthen its green economy transition through two overarching reforms to public sector management and governance: (i) government approval of the Strategic Framework on Green Economy, 2022–2030 and the long-term action plan for improving energy efficiency, conserving natural resources, reducing GHG emissions, improving access to green energy, and training the labor force in line with the green economy and gender-responsive generation of green jobs, and (ii) establishing an institutional framework to oversee strategy implementation. Reform will be deepened under subprogram 2. The government will analyze climate risk at project appraisal and selection, and incorporate adaptation and/or mitigation measures in climate-sensitive public investment projects. It will implement green budgeting methodology in selected ministries.

Philippines: Domestic Resource Mobilization Program. In anticipation of the proposed subprogram 1, the government submitted to Congress a bill that establishes mechanisms for carbon pricing to enable emission trading systems and other, nonmarket measures to transition to a low-carbon and climate-resilient economy. The government has mandated the Department of Finance to be a lead coordinating agency for fiscal policy on climate finance. The government further endorsed and submitted to Congress a bill to impose an excise tax on single-use plastic bags. It allocates excise tax revenue to improve local governments' solid waste management plans. This protects vulnerable groups such as the poor, women, the elderly, and children from waste and its serious health hazards, while the tax itself encourages citizens to use environmentally friendly alternatives to plastic bags. Carbon pricing and enforcement mechanisms for single-use plastic will be implemented in subprogram 2.

Table A2.5: Actions for low-carbon and climate-resilient public sector management and governance development

Action	Target Date
Support DMCs' formulation of fiscal and PFM policy actions.	31 Dec 2024
SG-PSMG will facilitate capacity development in DMCs by (i) developing guidance and technical notes to support the integration of climate functions into DMC fiscal and PFM policy; (ii) conducting workshops, seminars, and virtual courses to raise understanding about climate issues, natural hazards, and the required fiscal and PFM reform; and (iii) providing technical assistance to DMCs to update their PFM processes and procedures to smooth the implementation of reform.	
Develop high-quality climate policy-based loans and mainstream climate actions in the PSMG operational pipeline.	31 Dec 2024
SG-PSMG will work closely with regional departments and other sector offices to develop high-quality climate policy-based loans where feasible. To boost climate investment in PSMG and its alignment with the Paris Agreement, SG-PSMG will field diagnostic missions to selected DMCs to identify, prioritize, and sequence fiscal and PFM reforms required for the integration of climate functions. SG-PSMG will initiate diagnostics in selected countries to identify gaps between their climate objectives—national determined contributions, long-term strategies, and national action plans—and their fiscal and PFM circumstances and help DMCs to close these gaps through reform. Opportunities will be identified to collaborate with DMC private sector actors in energy and other sectors to raise climate-friendly investment to achieve resilient and low-carbon development.	
Explore opportunities to collaborate with other international finance institutions on capacity development in DMCs to achieve climate targets.	31 Dec 2024
Examples of opportunities include (i) planned collaboration with the IMF to assess the management of public investment in selected DMCs; (ii) an international conference scheduled for November 2023 on the importance of integrating climate functions into fiscal and PFM systems; and (iii) a conference on carbon pricing arranged for the government of Indonesia in October 2023 in collaboration with the IMF and the Council of Finance Ministers on Climate Action. SG-PSMG will participate in international forums to showcase PSMG work on climate.	

DMC = developing member country, IMF = International Monetary Fund, PFM = public financial management, PSMG = public sector management and governance, SG-PSMG = Public Sector Management and Governance Sector Office.

Source: Asian Development Bank.

6 TRANSPORT

Opportunities for low-carbon and climate-resilient development

Currently, the transport sector contributes significantly to GHG emissions. In 2019, it contributed 24% of direct CO_2 emissions from fuel combustion, with road transport accounting for 75% of it. In the same year, the vehicle market in Asia and the Pacific accounted for 48% of global sales. Asia's share of worldwide transport emissions is growing and expected to peak in 2040. The enhancement and expansion of transport systems will remain a significant driver of regional economic growth and competitiveness, as Asia is projected to produce 45% of global exports by 2050. To meet rising demand, ADB estimates that new transport infrastructure investment worth $557 billion will be needed annually. In parallel with tackling growth and development, a concerted effort is needed to achieve economic growth without adding transport GHG emissions.

In terms of mitigation, the transport sector will tackle low-carbon development by transforming the transport system through (i) rapid and significant reductions in demand (avoid), (ii) a shift in travel from high-carbon to low- and zero-carbon modes (shift), and (iii) the widescale adoption of technologies to decarbonize fuels and vehicles (improve). This strategy needs to be further examined for differentiated approaches across DMCs, to formulate relevant strategies based on their baseline emission levels and trajectory of emission increases.

In terms of adaptation, it is estimated that about $37 billion per year will be needed for climate-proofing to make new transport infrastructure resilient under future climate impacts. There is an urgent need to scale up support for countries' shifts toward delivering more resilient transport systems, which includes better asset management and scaling up adaptation. The financing requirement is estimated to equal 1.1%–2.1% of aggregate regional gross domestic product.

The most significant opportunities for climate-resilient and low-carbon development rely on a shift to rail and other mass transit systems, and on more efficient and decarbonized multimodal transport systems that are physically and digitally integrated. Crosscutting, multisector solutions will be critical to break out of sector silos and work across sectors—energy, urban, agriculture, finance, information technology, and public—to develop technologies for complex solutions. This will require increased climate financing, including from the private sector.

Barriers to low-carbon and climate-resilient development

Key challenges to climate-responsive development are (i) tackling climate change while continuing to fill large infrastructure deficits; (ii) coordinating policy action and strong political commitment to align with the Paris Agreement; (iii) providing adequate concessional climate finance, especially for lower-income countries; and (iv) overcoming institutional capacity constraints on implementing and financing clean infrastructure and integrated mobility. The transport sector receives 20%–25% of ADB annual funding commitments. To meet ADB's climate financing targets of $80 billion (or $100 billion ambition) in 2019–2030, the transport sector is expected to contribute 25%. Any increase in this contribution, however, depends on resource availability.

Good practices for low-carbon and climate-resilient development

The following projects showcase efforts to address climate mitigation and adaptation.

Policy, regulatory, and planning. Net-zero pathways for Mongolia takes a pilot approach developed to explore what policies, strategies, and infrastructure investments are needed to achieve net zero in the transport sector in Mongolia, with milestones set for the short, medium, and long term. These milestones can be used to inform the country partnership strategy and bring in potential financiers to enable net zero by the target date set by the government. In Indonesia, ADB developed a road map to build electric motorcycle charging infrastructure to support the government's ambition to accelerate the uptake of e-motorcycles for private and commercial purposes, including ride-hailing and delivery. This project mitigates climate change while alleviating air and noise pollution and reliance on fuel imports.

Private sector. Through the GreenCell Electric Bus Financing Project in India, ADB is providing to GreenCell Express Private Limited a $40 million financing package to develop 255 battery-powered electric buses to serve 5 million people annually on 56 intercity routes. It will enhance safety for passengers, especially women, through improved security features including panic buttons connected to command controls for immediate response. The financial package comprises a $20.5 million loan disbursed in Indian rupees from ADB ordinary capital resources, ADB's administration of a $14 million loan and a $325,000 grant from the Clean Technology Fund, and a $5.2 million grant from the Climate Innovation and Development Fund (CIDF) maintained by Goldman Sach and Bloomberg. ADB helped mobilize a parallel $20.5 million loan from the Asian Infrastructure Investment Bank. A defining feature of this project is that the CIDF grant will partly finance the decarbonization of 100 of 255 e-buses by deploying solar power-plus-battery energy storage systems, reducing CO_2 emissions by 6,355 tons per year. The whole project will reduce emissions by 14,780 tons per year.

Adaptation and resilience. ADB works with its Pacific DMCs to build and upgrade transport infrastructure to improve critical services and be more hazard and climate resilient. In Tonga, for instance, the Nuku'alofa Port Upgrade Project is rehabilitating degraded cargo wharves at Tonga's main port—a lifeline highly exposed to climate change and natural hazards, as demonstrated by a volcano eruption and consequent tsunami in 2022. ADB is contributing $55 million to the project in coordination with other bilateral development partners, including the Australian Infrastructure Financing Facility for the Pacific, which is cofinancing the project with $20 million. The project boosts port capacity to cope with projected demand over the next 20 years and strengthens its safety and climate resilience.

Mitigation. The South Commuter Railway Project in the Philippines will support the construction of the 54.6-kilometer (km) Blumentritt–Calamba section of the North–South Commuter Railway connecting Metro Manila and Calamba in Laguna Province, about 50 km south of Manila. The project will improve connectivity in the public transport network by connecting with all existing Light Rail Transit and Mass Rapid Transit lines in Metro Manila. It includes a connecting line to the planned Metro Manila Subway, which will improve connectivity by operating direct trains for passengers traveling from Calamba to Bonifacio Global City, Ortigas, and Quezon City on the Metro Manila Subway. The new railway line will provide affordable, reliable, and safe public transport, reduce GHG emissions, and cut travel time by half, to less than 1 hour.

In the PRC, Study on the Development of Green Ports and Shipping is TA to provide case studies of international best practice, policy recommendations, an investment road map, and knowledge sharing. Further, TA will promote innovation in port operations and inland waterway shipping by introducing new technology to power port equipment and vessels with clean energy and reduce GHG emissions and other pollution. It will use green hydrogen or other clean energy applications in ports and electric or alternative solutions for vessels.

The Davao Public Transport Modernization Project will modernize public bus transport in Davao City, the third largest city in the Philippines, with modern electric buses and Euro-5 standard diesel buses, standardized operations, and an intelligent transport system for bus operation. It will rationalize 670 km of bus routes into 30 routes carrying 800,000 passengers per day by establishing bus operation concessions with private bus operators using performance-based contracts, 1,000 bus stops, five bus depots, three bus terminals, dedicated bus lanes, pedestrian crossings and sidewalks, a control center, an automatic fare collection system, and bus priority traffic signaling under an intelligent transport system.

In India, the Delhi–Meerut Regional Rapid Transit System Investment Project will use a $1 billion loan to build a 82 km Delhi–Meerut regional rapid transit system, the first of three priority rail corridors the country plans in its integrated transport network. Urban land use for transit-oriented development will be linked with land value capture financing. An ADB $427 million loan for Chongqing Integrated Logistics Demonstration in the PRC supports a modern and efficient multimodal logistics system in the Yangtze River Economic Belt and Silk Road Economic Belt, which include the Chongqing and Nanpeng logistics park; Yangtze River inland waterway roll-on, roll-off operations; and a logistics information system.

Table A2.6: Actions for low-carbon and climate-resilient transport development

Action	Target Date
Establish accelerated low-carbon transport transition projects and programs, strengthen partnerships, and enhance access to public and private resources. (i) Design and expedite projects under work programs and upstream activities to meet cumulative 2030 climate financing and result targets. (ii) Develop a new ADB-wide program to accelerate a low-carbon transition in transport. (iii) Increase private sector investment in transport. (iv) Increase cofinancing with external finance sources. (v) Improve collaboration and coordination among multilateral development banks and with bilateral development partners on Paris Agreement alignment, climate issues, and the implementation of nationally determined contributions for transport, and promote regional collaboration and coordination through the Greater Mekong Subregion, Central Asia Regional Economic Cooperation, South Asia Subregional Economic Cooperation, and the Bay of Bengal Initiative for Multisectoral Technical and Economic Cooperation. *Consolidate transport sector TA for approval by the first quarter of 2024. Expedite approvals for 5 programs by 2025 and 10 programs by 2030, or cumulative $25 billion in climate financing.*[a]	Ongoing
Strengthen policy, strategy, and institutional support. (i) Help developing member countries (DMCs) develop low-carbon sector pathways or similar strategies covering policies, programs, and investment plans. (ii) Support the development of climate-smart infrastructure design standards such as nature-based solutions and green infrastructure design. (iii) Support Type 1 climate-proof transport projects to ensure that critical infrastructure is resilient under current and future climate risks. (iv) Assess upstream climate vulnerabilities in DMC transport systems to target transport projects for Type 2 adaptation projects for both development and climate-resilient outcomes. (v) Advise DMCs on creating supportive policy environments to drive private sector investment in transport. *Consolidate transport sector TA for approval by the first quarter of 2024. Include in country sector assessments for programs analysis for low-carbon pathways, and prepare five high-level policy briefs by 2030. Assess climate risk vulnerability in DMCs to target Type 2 adaptation for three transport projects by 2025.*	Ongoing

continued on next page

Table continued

Action	Target Date
Improve knowledge solutions and capacity development for low-carbon and climate-resilient transport.	Ongoing
(i) Engage with the Climate Change and Sustainable Development Department and the Budget, Personnel, and Management Systems Department to recruit and allocate climate specialists to be transport sector climate change focal points. (ii) Implement targeted and demand-driven training and awareness-raising programs for climate change in DMC transport sectors. (iii) Train sector experts on the joint development of low-carbon pathways as possible inputs into DMC nationally determined contributions and long-term strategies. (iv) Provide technical assistance linked to the project pipeline to design multisector solutions combining agricultural value chains, urban systems, and information technology—and encompassing advanced clean technology, greening railways, logistics chains, system electrification, e-mobility solutions, optimized fleet utilization, green urban systems, transit-oriented development, digital transport solutions, and the private sector—to finance technologies for complex solutions, operation and maintenance, and a logistics center. (v) Link to the operations pipeline targeted knowledge products to inform and advise DMCs on long-term transport investment planning for a low-carbon pathway and development targets. Monitor progress toward targets and decarbonization by subsector.	
Deliver by 2030 upstream knowledge-based solutions and components targeting five pipeline operations that contribute to low-carbon pathways.	
Enhance and expand internal capacity in transport.	Ongoing
Increase transport staffing and resources to strengthen capacity to achieve higher deliverables than the targeted $25 billion by 2030.	
Adopt product-agnostic approaches to identifying high-impact climate interventions in the transport sector.	Ongoing
Require all sector teams to undertake sector diagnostics with a view to identifying potential investments, sovereign and nonsovereign, to foster greater collaboration across sovereign teams and the Private Sector Operations Department.	

[a] The $25 billion ambition by 2030 contributes to ADB's $100 billion ambition. The transport sector received 20% of ADB funding commitment on average in 2019–2022.

Source: Asian Development Bank.

7 WATER AND URBAN DEVELOPMENT

Opportunities for low-carbon and climate-resilient development

Asian cities currently produce 75% of regional carbon emissions. By 2030, more than 55% of the population of Asia and the Pacific will live in urban areas, driving up demand for urban services. If urban areas continue along the same growth trajectory, Asian cities could contribute more than half of the rise in global GHG emissions over the next 20 years. At the same time, Asia is home to 99 of the world's 100 cities most threatened by environmental and climate risks.

ADB works with cities and towns in Asia and the Pacific to bring transformative change by promoting resilient, low-carbon urban development and the application of circular economy approaches.

Urban planning and design. ADB works with municipalities to strengthen urban planning systems, reduce energy demand, and enable more sustainable mobility options such as public transit-oriented development and facilitated land value capture. Cities benefit from ADB support to promote risk-informed urban planning and discourage development in the areas most exposed to natural hazards and climate change. ADB promotes urban greening to reduce heat island effects, improve air quality, and mitigate increasingly frequent and severe heat waves.

Integrated urban services. ADB works with water and sanitation service providers to manage demand, reduce nonrevenue water, and improve energy efficiency. ADB investment projects support water supply, wastewater, and stormwater management in a holistic and integrated manner for long-term water security, resilience, and reliability. Nature-positive solutions to reduce flooding are being adopted, notably "sponge city" approaches to capture storm runoff for groundwater recharge and other uses. ADB-financed investments in sanitation reduce potent GHG emissions and protect water resources by improving management for the entire sanitation service chain, from containment to disposal and reuse. Increasingly, ADB promotes opportunities for wastewater reuse and energy capture from sludge treatment.

Open dumps are the third largest source of methane globally. ADB helps municipalities improve solid waste management by promoting waste segregation at source to remove organic waste and other recyclables from the waste stream and improve final disposal in modern landfills that manage leachate and methane emissions. Through nonsovereign and other investments, ADB supports waste-to-energy investments for heat and electricity toward reducing waste volume, if feedstock for combustion reflects prudent priorities in the order of waste management.

Emerging areas. To serve the region's growing urban population, ADB supports the provision of housing that is affordable, climate and disaster resilient, and in line with green building standards. Globally, residential buildings are among the largest sources of GHG emissions. ADB invests in climate-resilient tourism infrastructure and improved solid waste and wastewater systems, which create livelihoods for local communities, conserve natural and cultural heritage resources, and enhance the sustainability of tourism development and operations. Measuring and monitoring impacts, ADB promotes sustainable and resilient tourism development in the region.

Financing and private sector participation. ADB works with municipalities and utilities to strengthen their financial sustainability by expanding revenue mobilization and facilitating access to climate financing. This better enables them to make the low-carbon investments critically needed to increase the quality, reliability, and resilience of urban services. ADB promotes private sector participation in the delivery of urban services to improve operational efficiency and sustainability. Disaster risk financing instruments such as climate change bonds and city disaster insurance pools are also supported by ADB.

Barriers to low-carbon and climate-resilient development

Key barriers to promoting resilient and low-carbon urban development in Asia and the Pacific are outlined below.

Governance challenges. Institutional silos challenge the implementation of integrated urban planning and management approaches, splitting key subsector functions across different government agencies. Urban plans are ideally developed in conjunction with, for example, transport investment plans to promote optimal urban development patterns and ensure adequate access to sustainable mobility services to meet growing demand. Metropolitan areas pose additional challenges when climate resilience and mitigation action requires coordination between multiple local governments. Cities critically need tools and guidance to downscale NDCs and thus develop city climate action plans, regulate appropriately to allow cities to manage climate risks, ensure that fiscal transfer mechanisms incentivize city climate action, and engage with the private sector.

Urban growth in Asia and the Pacific is often unplanned or contrary to plan as municipalities struggle to enforce zoning and other development controls. Inappropriate development occurs in hazard-prone areas such as floodplains, and natural waterways and wetlands are drained and infilled, exacerbating vulnerability to flood risk. Similarly, many regulations, building codes, and other infrastructure design standards are outdated and unsuitable to meet today's climate challenges. Building codes do not consider current and future climate risks. Engineering design standards for gray infrastructure fail in many countries to consider nature-based solutions, which constrains their options for flexible and cost-effective adaptation.

Insufficient finance. Low-carbon and climate-resilient urban development is constrained by insufficient finance. Many local governments and utilities in the region struggle to mobilize finance because they suffer low financial sustainability and creditworthiness. In weak enabling environments, managed tariffs are set below cost-recovery, deterring private investment in urban services. Municipalities and other urban service providers thus rely heavily on government transfers that are often insufficient to cover operation and maintenance costs, let alone fund necessary capital investment.

Financial preparedness and capacity to respond to disasters is low, and cities struggle to secure resources to fund timely recovery efforts such as the restoration of critical infrastructure, delivery of services, and support for livelihoods.

Limited knowledge and capacity. Municipalities and urban service providers often lack access to natural hazard and climate change data or capacity to comprehensively assess climate change and disaster risk to inform urban planning and infrastructure investment.

Good practices for low-carbon and climate-resilient development

A number of good practice examples highlight ADB efforts to promote low-carbon and climate-resilient urban development.

Coastal Towns Climate Resilience Project. This project in Bangladesh is ADB's first Type 2 adaptation project in the urban sector. With 90% climate adaptation financing, the project will strengthen climate resilience in vulnerable coastal towns and capacity in local *pourashavas* and the Local Government and Engineering Department. The project has three outputs. First is to improve municipal infrastructure and essential services for climate and disaster resilience and spur local economic development to strengthen towns' adaptive capacity. Second is to enhance livelihoods and thus boost capacity in vulnerable households to deal with climate shocks in six towns with high poverty rates. Third is to strengthen institutional capacity, governance, and climate-awareness toward building climate resilience with urban development plans informed by climate and disaster risk, increased knowledge and capacity to implement nature-based solutions, and strengthened capacity to allocate municipal budgets based on risk and performance.

Jilin Yanji Low-Carbon Climate-Resilient Healthy City Project. This project in the PRC systemically integrates gray infrastructure, including for transport, and green "sponge city" infrastructure to enhance resilience. The project is financing the first bus rapid transit (BRT) line in the city, toward creating high-density, mixed-use, and pedestrian-friendly center areas around BRT stations. It integrates nonmotorized transport lanes and facilities along the corridor, providing small roads and river greenways to ensure safe and pleasant pedestrian and bicycle access to BRT stations while promoting low-carbon urban mobility and physical activity to enhance public health. Project greenways are designed as sponge city green infrastructure to enhance climate resilience and urban livability. The project will improve water supply and wastewater management systems to ensure safe and climate-resilient access to clean water.

Mainstreaming Climate Change Resilience in Asia and the Pacific. This regional TA is to embed resilience in the design of ADB-financed water operations through advisory support, knowledge sharing, and capacity building. TA finances high-quality international experts on climate change, smart water management, and institutional reform through framework contracts that ADB staff can employ to plan and design water projects for outcomes that maximize resilience. TA supports rapid capacity building in water entities in Asia and the Pacific through twinning partnerships between water operators, and through the Asia Pacific Resilience Hub.

Table A2.7: Actions for low-carbon and climate-resilient water and urban development

Action	Target Date
Strengthen planning and design to support low-carbon and climate-resilient urban development.	Ongoing
(i) Generate greater upstream engagement with developing member country (DMC) counterparts at the national and city level, including finance ministries, to identify priority investments to shift urban development to lower-carbon and more resilient development trajectories, such as through the application of adaptive pathway approaches, and conduct upstream climate assessment before and during the project concept stage to mainstream climate mitigation and adaptation opportunities. (ii) Bring DMC counterparts up to speed on climate financing to get more buy-in and climate-financing proposals from the government. (iii) Further integrate subsectors in urban planning to identify synergies such as transit-oriented development. (iv) Promote participatory urban planning. (v) Strengthen risk-informed land-use planning. (vi) Promote digital technologies such as building and city information modeling and digital twins in urban planning, construction, and operation. *Conceptualize and prepare five Type 2 adaptation projects by 2025. Increase the number of projects using or supporting urban and land-use planning informed by climate risk, transit-oriented development, and urban planning frameworks to 5 by 2025 and 10 by 2030.*	
Support urban policy and governance reform.	Ongoing
(i) Help DMC clients review and update relevant policies and regulations and design incentives to ensure that climate considerations are adequately reflected. (ii) Work with entities to review and update design standards and building codes to reflect rising climate and disaster risk, promote energy efficiency, and enable the mainstreaming of nature-based solutions. (iii) Promote planning approaches that better coordinate sector agencies with local, regional, and national agencies. (iv) Work with other partners to consider adopting existing climate tools and approaches. *Support at least five policy and/or governance reforms through various loan modalities or technical assistance by the end of 2025.*	
Promote financial innovations to mobilize more climate finance for urban development.	Ongoing
(i) Improve the enabling environment to promote greater investment in urban infrastructure and services by the public and private sector. (ii) Work with municipalities and utilities to improve their financial sustainability and creditworthiness. (iii) Promote innovative financing approaches such as climate bonds, carbon credits, disaster risk insurance, de-risking mechanisms, and blended finance to expand access to climate finance. *Commit financing by the end of 2025 to at least five sovereign or nonsovereign projects with innovative private sector participation elements and/or support to domestic resource mobilization in water and urban development with climate resilience and/or mitigation features.*	

continued on next page

Table continued

Action	Target Date
Improve knowledge and capacity building to design and implement low-carbon and climate-resilient urban development actions.	Ongoing
(i) Build capacity to undertake risk-informed planning, analyze the cost-effectiveness of resilience measures, and identify opportunities to promote decarbonization and resilience in the design and delivery of urban services. (ii) Make available the data and tools necessary to support more informed decision-making. (iii) Exploit co-benefit arguments for climate action likely to resonate with clients: the clear benefits of low-carbon approaches for both greenhouse gas emissions and air pollution, for example, in terms of local environmental improvement, improved quality of life, and reduced health-care costs. (iv) Provide technical support to ensure that climate is mainstreamed in project design and investment, including through engagement with the ministry of finance to build its awareness and capacity. (v) Share knowledge and good practices for low-carbon urban resilience such as nature-based solutions, innovative financing mechanisms, and digitization. *Support by the end of 2025 at least five water utilities or city governments in their preparation of decarbonization and resilience road maps.*	
Enhance internal capacity in the Water Sector Group.	Ongoing
(i) Ensure that staff and other resources are available to mainstream climate in water and urban sector operations. (ii) Streamline quality control in climate risk assessment and adaptation with support from One ADB team members. (iii) Develop staff capacity in climate change. (iv) Ensure that all ADB urban and water sector operations align with the Paris Agreement. (v) Lead the development of a consistent approach across ADB to estimating climate finance for water and urban development operations, learn the practices of multilateral development banks and other peer organizations, and regularly take stock of projects. *Deliver by the end of 2025 climate and water training to selected staff in water and urban development and in agriculture, fisheries, and natural resources. Ensure ADB presence and inputs at five climate conferences by the end of 2025.*	
Adopt product-agnostic approaches to identifying high-impact climate interventions in water and urban development.	Ongoing
Require all sector teams to undertake sector diagnostics with a view to identifying potential investments, sovereign and nonsovereign, to foster greater collaboration across sovereign teams and the Private Sector Operations Department.	

Source: Asian Development Bank.

Printed in the USA
CPSIA information can be obtained
at www.ICGtesting.com
LVHW060923191124
797022LV00012B/94